A Map of Absence

An Anthology of Palestinian Writing on the Nakba

Edited by
Atef Alshaer

SAQI

Published 2019 by Saqi Books

ISBN 978 0 86356 990 6
eISBN 978 0 86356 995 1

A full CIP record for this book is available from the British Library.

Printed and bound in Great Britain by Clays Ltd, Elcograf S.p.A.

CONTENTS

INTRODUCTION

Atef Alshaer

CREATIVE writing is a process of engaging with human passions and concerns. However profoundly writing might be embedded within a particular tradition, it is always in a dialogue with present, lived experiences. In the case of Palestine, literature has been a source of national rebirth, documentation and emancipation, engaging with a burdened reality and an ongoing tragedy. This is encapsulated by the Nakba, literally, 'the catastrophe' – the moment in 1948 when almost half the population of Palestine were driven from their homes. Villages were ransacked, cities were levelled.

The Nakba of Palestine is commemorated each year on 15 May. It is on this same day that the foundation of Israel has been celebrated annually since 1948. For Palestinians, the Nakba is a day blackened by the memory of the destruction that Israel inflicted on them, robbing them of their homeland and leaving in its stead loss, insecurity and instability. It is also a bewildering reminder that one's nation still exists – in all but name.

* * *

At the beginning of the twentieth century, Palestinians, like most Arabs, used poetry as their principal form of artistic expression. Arabic poetry has historically been performative, giving it a power and wide audience in the days before written literacy and the internet made it easier to spread the word. This performance aspect facilitated the memorising of poetry and thus its repetition in a variety of everyday contexts.

We often associate spoken Palestinian poetry from the past century with protests, typically against colonialism and the ravaging of Arab land and people. This intense desire to write and perform drove poets of that era to adapt and hone their literary skills, and a movement towards free verse gathered pace. They were transcending the restrictions of the old formulae and establishing new poetic aesthetics. Moreover, their contact with European literary traditions, mainly British and French, encouraged them to explore the short story and novel forms in Arabic for the first time. But that is not to say that their work was no longer evocative of earlier, classical Arabic traditions. In particular, the classical poetic tradition, which extends from the fifth century to the thirteenth century covering the pre-Islamic, the Umayyad and the Abbasid periods, informs the language of Mahmoud Darwish and other Palestinian writings. Indeed, all modern literary Arabic writing is in one form or another indebted to Classical Arabic literature and the spirit of innovation that it represented.

Palestinian literature emerged in the context of resisting the colonisation of the writers' land. This necessitated the assertion of historical continuity, the statements of an ancient community linked to the broader Arab world, sharing with it a long-founded literary heritage as well as social and cultural norms. Yet with time, Palestinian literature developed in reaction to the internationalism and modernisation that several literary schools in the Arab world and beyond advanced. It evolved to transcend strict nationalist loyalties, even critiquing tribal forms of nationalism. Increasingly freed from ideology and its fetters, it was newly equipped to express the plight of humankind – all of our struggles, frustrations, insecurities and aspirations – in fluid, and sometimes subversive, ways.

Yet it would be a gross simplification to suggest that a linear path has been followed. While this anthology takes a chronological view of Palestinian literature, starting in the 1930s, the writing here remains preoccupied with the same unanswered questions concerning the dispossession of the Palestinian people and their conditions of being occupied. After all, the quest for Palestinian freedom has yet to bear fruit.

* * *

This collection consists of poems, short stories, excerpts from longer fiction and memoirs of the Nakba. Some of the texts have been translated from Arabic while others were originally written in English. A solid and enduring constituency of Palestinians are writing in English, in ways that have brought the Palestinian tragedy to the attention of the wider world in candid and eloquent ways. Among their number are the Palestinian scholar and thinker Edward Said, Salman Abu Sitta, Ghada Karmi, Ramzy Baroud and Fady Joudah. The selected texts speak to different Palestinian communities, including those within historic Palestine, those in the Occupied Territories and the Palestinian diaspora.

Also presented here are works by authors who have had intimate connections with Palestine, such as the Lebanese novelist Elias Khoury. Finally, we also celebrate the work of emerging writers in Palestine, such as Amira Sakalla, whose work is published here for the first time.

We trace Palestinian writing over almost ninety years. With a certain amount of generalisation acknowledged, we can divide that span into three phases. The first extends from the 1930s to the 1950s, the second from the 1960s to the beginnings of the 1990s, and the third from 1993 until today. While the fate of Palestine remains the constant concern for its writers, each of these periods has its own defining characteristics. The first unfolds under Zionist attacks and the mass displacement of Palestinian refugees. The second covers the time when Palestinians formed a national movement and resisted the colonisation of their land. The third sees Palestinians debating the possibility, or impossibility, of peaceful resolution with Israel, following the Oslo Accords of 1993.

The early generation of Palestinian poets composed poetry in classical form, using traditional, predictable patterns of rhyme, rhythm and metre. This gave way to free verse, particularly from the 1950s onwards. Despite becoming less rigidly structured, Palestinian poetry maintained an internal musicality, and was thus well suited to recitation at political protests. The voices of classical Palestinian poets, including Ibrahim Tuqan, Abdel Rahim Mahmoud and Abu Salma al-Karmi, typify the literature of the decades from the 1930s to the 1950s.

The anthology begins with these voices. Ibrahim Tuqan belongs to a movement who, in the 1920s and 1930s, observed British and Zionist stratagems with their own eyes. His poem *My Homeland* is a historic national anthem for Palestine. It is a tender love song for its landscape and fauna and flora, and a statement of defence and defiance against the colonisers. His other most noted poem, *The Bloody Thursday*, commemorates the hanging by the British of three Palestinian nationalists, for taking part in the revolt against Britain's repression of the Palestinians in 1936. The poem galvanised Palestinians and stirred them to resist, particularly as it was soon put into song. It was one of the early poems that served as a statement of mobilisation as well as the register of a collective Palestinian memory, while garnering wide Arab sympathy and support.

Sacrifice and devotion to the land become significant themes in early Palestinian literature, commemorating, re-creating and reclaiming the homeland through language that evokes nostalgia, loss and resistance all in the same breath. Other poets from the 1930s to the 1950s who intensify this dynamic are Abu Salma Al-Karmi and Abdel Al-Rahim Mahmoud, who was killed by the

British. Avowedly nationalist, yet rarely dogmatic or inhuman towards their oppressors, they paved a way for others to be sensitive as well as passionate.

The short story began to gain ground in Arabic literature in the mid-twentieth century. In her tale *Man and His Clock*, Samira Azzam revisits Palestine before the Nakba and reflects on an ordinary life with all its blessings and bitter disappointments. Through this reflection, Azzam demonstrates the versatility of Palestinians and their dedication to modernisation. If the Nakba is present in this text, it is in gestures and hints. The pain of a nation is symbolised by the individual, for example the old man's son, who dies on the rails beneath a steam train, introduced to the region by the British. Azzam inspired Palestinian writers to revisit the past as a way of talking about the present.

The novelist and writer Ghassan Kanafani provides a bridge between the first and second generations. His poignant narratives epitomise the Palestinian experience in its most elemental form, against the backdrop of his personal story as a refugee forced to leave for the unknown. A story included in this anthology, *A Present for the Holiday*, describes the hardships and loneliness of the Palestinians as they become refugees. Palestinians are abandoned, left to fend for themselves, receiving meagre hand-outs from international organisations: 'I remember nothing except the cold, and the ice that manacled my fingers and the can of soup.'

Kanafani developed his literary techniques to employ modernist and postmodernist sensibilities in his depiction of fragmentary and unsettling situations. His methods included the use of streams of consciousness, making him less dependent on chronology and plot. He was free to explore psychological issues and individual behaviours. Kanafani's characters, though tormented and existentially confused, are often revolutionaries seeking a solution: an end to their sudden exile and displacement. He used a wide cast of characters, allowing him to reflect on class differences, labour exploitation and political marginalisation in line with his own political activism.

The second generation of writers includes Tawfiq Ziad, Samih al-Qassim, Fadwa Tuqan and Mahmoud Darwish, among others. The places where they recited their poems were concentrated near the sites of Palestinian struggle, whether inside Palestine or outside in the diaspora. Poetry spread first through word of mouth, gained momentum through recitation in rallies, and was later distributed and preserved on cassettes. (Each generation uses the technology of its time to disseminate writing – today's Palestinian poets have taken to social media.) Rather than speaking only to Palestinians familiar with the struggle, Palestinian writing from the 1960s onwards began to engage with people less familiar with the politics behind the experiences.

Palestinians began to write in broader terms. This reflected the widening of Palestinian identity, as Palestinians were first forced to move away into new communities, sometimes abroad, and establish a diaspora. Trauma, ordinary struggles and snippets of daily life and habits became important sources of poetic content and composition. Writers occupied themselves with the complexities of life under occupation and became less embroiled in discourses of nationalist mobilisation.

During the 1960s and 1970s, certain talented Palestinian poets came to occupy a prominent place in the Arab literary scene, influencing Palestinian literature for decades to come. They were working from refugee camps in Lebanon, Syria and Jordan, and from within historic Palestine that became Israel, and elsewhere. Writers also moved from one country to another, as they were mostly allied to the newly formed Palestine Liberation Organisation and subject to its stateless condition. This is the case for the poets Mahmoud Darwish, Ahmad Dahbour, Muin Bseiso, Mourid Barghouti and others.

Nationalist poetry flourished at sites where there were direct confrontations with the Israeli occupation, such as in Lebanon, where the PLO was stationed from 1970 to 1982. This poetry extolled the virtues of resistance and celebrated Palestine and its nationalist cause. Other novelists and writers were diagnosing the more internal problems of Palestine. In general, throughout their history, Palestinian writers tended to embrace nationalism as a means to unite their people and galvanise them towards the liberation of Palestine. But they were also critical of certain aspects of the struggle, and of archaic forms of behaviour prevalent in the greater Arab world, including patriarchy and dictatorship.

Outside Palestine, other novelists of this time, such as Jabra Ibrahim Jabra, identified Palestinians as people in need of cultural reformation and refinement. Culture and art were seen as essential to national and universal healing, and to human development. This strand of thought was common among the Arab inheritors of the nineteenth-century An-Nahda, or 'renaissance', such as Constantine Zurayq, who popularised the term 'Nakba' in reference to Palestine and investigated its roots.

Inside Palestine, the rise of writers such as Emile Habibi, Mahmoud Darwish, Samih al-Qassim, Fadwa Tuqan and others from the 1960s onwards spoke directly to Palestinians, with writing that knows of their pains and aspirations. Yet these authors, particularly Mahmoud Darwish, came to universalise Palestine. Their literature reflects the Palestinian sense of displacement and struggle; it counters oppression with beauty and magnanimity, and thus still strikes a chord with those outside the country and the cause. Theirs is a poetry of commemorative healing, as much as it is of resistance and defiance; an outcry for justice and truth in the face of powers that have denied them both.

Palestinian writers who came of age in the 1960s were to define Palestinian literature, looming large over the literary scene for decades to come. They became significant political and literary figures, through whose writings Palestinian identity is assessed. They came to exemplify a genre in world literature called 'resistance literature', as they were seen as significant revolutionary voices standing for the downtrodden, with Palestine serving as a litmus test for international solidarity.

Mahmoud Darwish (1941–2008) is particularly important, as his poetic vocation covers nearly six decades of the Palestinian struggle. He became the most eloquent voice of Palestinian refugees, his work anchored in the Palestinian predicament. At the same time, humanism and universalism were a part of his message from the start of the 1960s, when he wrote his stirring poem *Record, I am an Arab*. Over time Darwish's poetry evolved away from the directly nationalist, and this in part explains why he was able to find such a broad audience and bring in individuals who had not previously associated with the Palestinian cause. The same can be said for Palestinian poetry more broadly at this time, which, though committed to local justice, also encompassed appreciation of the predicament of peoples all over the world.

The writings of the Palestinian-American thinker Edward Said also amplified the voice of Palestine on an international stage, particularly from the late 1970s to the end of his life in 2003. A writer with an exceptional command of the English language and the cultures that use it, Said began to educate the West about Palestine, its Nakba of 1948 and the on-going effects of the catastrophe. His work made conspicuous virtues of knowledge and style, but also sincerity of emotion and expression. Said inspired Palestinian writers to be bold in defending Palestine and linking its plight to other struggles, so that the entire world could have a stake in the liberation of Palestine.

The third generation of writers, writing after the Oslo Accords in 1993, are prepared to challenge elitism as well as questions of national identity. The Accords, ostensibly a whole suite of agreements between the Palestine Liberation Organisation and Israel, perplexed Palestinian writers and the wider community. Although some hailed the agreement as a political breakthrough, many others believed that, rather than pave the way towards an independent Palestinian state, they had effectively created a Palestinian-administered Israeli occupation. Their literature examines in depth the political contradictions of Palestinian life and the state in general. The memoirs of Palestinian writers from this era are riddled with agonising incongruities and dilemmas, deepening their understanding of commitment to Palestine, but increasing their anxiety over its fate. In new ways they revisit the hopes and aspirations of earlier writers.

Palestinian literature from the 1990s onwards is rich in experimentation and expressionism. It is no longer a literature of direct resistance that uses militant language, even though this continues to be found in the younger generation's writings. When literature documents, it does so through details; through minutiae, big subjects are examined. This can be found in many Palestinian memoirs and novels, such as those of the prolific writer Ibrahim Nasrallah, of Salman Abu Sitta and Ghada Karmi, all of whom visit a pre-1948 past. Therein, the landscape of Palestine is a ground for dramatic human happenings, stretching back in time; life under the Ottoman Empire or the British Mandate might provide them with useful lenses through which to view the concept of their nation. This narrative comes severely and irreparably to a halt with the 1948 Nakba, leaving a void and silence that continues to haunt Palestinian lives.

Palestinian writers from this new generation, such as Adania Shibli, explore Palestine philosophically. Abstract questions of time and space are examined in relation to the realities of the Palestinian past and present. Shibli chronicles the long Palestinian journey of creative writing as one that continues to inspire, even when the Palestinian struggle seems to freeze in time. Her writing is particularly marked with the absence of subjective presence, so that writing itself is an ambiguous activity, loaded with collective angst and personal loss. It occupies a realm of irreconcilable inner forces, fed by conflict and tension, inflicted with anxiety and unrealisable nostalgia. Yet Shibli extols writing in such conditions as an act of continuity. Reflecting on Azzam's aforementioned *Man and His Alarm Clock*, Shibli writes:

> The text, in turn, had engraved in my soul a deep sense of yearning for all that was – including the tragic – normal and banal, to a degree that I could no longer accept the marginalised, minor life to which we've been exiled since 1948, during which our existence turned into a 'problem'.

* * *

There is hardly any writing tradition in the modern world that follows one linear path. Palestinian writing offers no exception to this. Yet the Nakba cannot cease to be a seminal event in Palestinian lives. While the work in this anthology attempts to reconstruct, describe and reflect on it, it also constantly invents methods of expression and telling. Therefore, while the catastrophe of the Nakba continues, so do the Palestinian writers' efforts to recover their history and convey its significance. They inhabit their own stories not only as victims of a major historical injustice, but also as agents in the development of Palestine – the idea and the living reality.

The writing here may focus on a single theme, but the evidence examined and the conclusions drawn reflect a variety of experiences and fluctuating emotions. The reader will discover that Palestinian literature, while connected to common political events and sentiments, can be surprisingly individual, often innovative and keenly mindful of aesthetic and literary developments outside its own territory. Nowhere has the voice of Palestine resonated more powerfully than in the literature of Palestinians.

IBRAHIM TUQAN

My Homeland

My homeland, My homeland
Majesty and beauty, sublimity and splendour,
Are in your hills, are in your hills,

Life and deliverance, pleasure and hope
Are in your air, are in your air
When will I see you? When will I see you?
Secure and prosperous
Victorious and honoured
Will I see you in your eminence
Reaching the stars, reaching the stars?
My homeland, my homeland

My homeland, my homeland
Our youth will not tire, until your independence
Or they will die, or they will die
We will drink from the cup of death and never be to our enemies
Like slaves, like slaves
We do not want, we do not want
An eternal humiliation nor a miserable life,
An eternal humiliation nor a miserable life,
We do not want, but we will bring back
Our great glory, our great glory
My homeland, my homeland

My homeland, My homeland
The sword and the pen, not talk nor quarrel,
Are our symbols, are our symbols
Our glory and our covenant and a duty to be faithful
Arouse us, arouse us
Our glory, Our glory
Is an honourable cause and a waving banner
Is an honourable cause and a waving banner
O, behold you in your eminence
Victorious over your enemies
My homeland, My homeland.

Excerpt from Red Tuesday

When your ill-fated star rose
And heads swayed in the nooses,
Minaret calls and church bells lamented,
Night was grim, and day was gloomy.
Storms and emotions began to rage
And death roamed about, snatching lives way,
And the eternal spade dug deep into the soil
To return them to its petrified heart.

It was a day that looked back upon past ages
And asked, 'Has the world seen a day like me?'
'Yes,' answered another day. 'I'll tell you
All about the iniquitous Inquisition courts.
I have indeed witnessed strange and odd events.
But yours are misfortunes and catastrophes,
The like of which in injustice I have never seen.
Ask then other days, among which many are abominable.'

Dragging its heavy fetters, a day responded,
History being one of its witnesses:
'Look at slaves, white and black,
Owned by anyone who had the money.
They were humans bought and sold, but are now free.
Yet time has gone backwards, as far as I can see ...
And those who forbade the purchase and sale of slaves
Are now hawking the free.'

A day wrapped in a dark-coloured robe
Staggered under the delirium of suffering
And said, 'No, yours is a much lesser pain than mine.
For I lost my young men on the hills of Aley
And witnessed the Butcher's deeds, inducing bloody tears.
Woe to him, how unjust! But ...
I've never met as terrible a day as you are.
Go, then. Perhaps you're the Day of Resurrection.'

The Day is considered abominable by all past ages
And eyes will keep looking at it with dismay.
How unfair the decisions of the course have been,
The least of which are proverbial in injustice.
The homeland is going to perdition, without hope.
The disease has no medicine but dignified pride
That renders one immune, and whoever is marked by it
Will end up dying undefeated.
Everyone hoped for [the High Commissioner's] early pardon,
And we prayed that he could never be distressed.
If this was the extent of his tenderness and kindness,
Long live His Majesty and long live His excellency!
The mail carried details of what had been put in a nutshell.

Please, stop supplicating and begging.
The give-and-take of entreaties is tantamount to death.
Therefore, take the shortest way of life.

The mail was overloaded with pleading, but nothing changed.
We humbled ourselves and wrote in various forms.
Our loss is both in souls and in money,
And our dignity is – alas – in rage.
You see what's happening, yet ask what's next?
Deception, like madness, is of many kind.
A humiliated soul, even if created to be all eyes,
Will not be able to see – far from it.
How is it possible for the voice of complaint to be heard,
And for the tears of mourning to be of any avail?
The rocks that felt our plea broke up in sympathy.
Yet, on reaching their hearts, our plea was denied.
No wonder, for some rocks burst with gushing fountains,
But their hearts like graves, with no feeling.
Don't ever seek favours from someone
You tried and found to be heartless.

All translated by Issa J. Boullata

GHASSAN KANAFANI

A Present for the Holiday

I was sleeping very late. There is a Chinese writer whose name is Sun Tsi and who lived hundreds of years before Christ. I was very attracted by him. He relieved my weariness and held my attention. (However, all that is beside the point of what I am going to write about.) He wrote that war is subterfuge and that victory is in anticipating everything and making your enemy expect nothing. He wrote that war is surprise. He wrote that war is an attack on ideals. He wrote …

But all that is beside the point …

I was sleeping very late and the telephone rang very early. The voice that came from the other end was completely refreshed and awake, almost joyful and proud. There were no feelings of guilt in its modulations. Half asleep, I said to myself: this is a man who gets up early. Nothing troubles him at night. The night had been rainy, with thunder and strong winds. Do you see what men do in times like this, the men who are marching in the early darkness to build for us an honour unstained by the mud? The night was rainy, and this man, at the other end of the line …

But all this is also beside the point.

He said to me: 'I have an idea. We'll collect toys for the children and send them to the refugees in Jordan, to the camps. You know, these are holidays now.'

I was half asleep. The camps. Those stains on the forehead of our weary morning, lacerations brandished like flags of defeat, billowing by chance above the plains of mud and dust and compassion. I had been teaching that day in one of those camps. One of the young students, called Darwish, sold cakes after school was out and I had chased him in between the tents and the mud and the sheets of tin and the puddles in order to get him into the evening class. His hair was short and curly and always wet. He was very bright and he wrote the best creative compositions in the class. If he had found something for himself to eat that day, his genius knew no bounds. It was a big camp. They called it ...

But that too is beside the point.

The man at the other end of the line said to me: 'It's an excellent idea, don't you think? You'll help us. We want a news campaign in the papers, you know.' Even though I was half asleep, just the right phrases leapt to mind: 'Mr So-and-So spent his New Year holiday collecting toys for the refugees. High society women will distribute them in the camps.' The camps are muddy, and dresses this season are short and the boots are white. Just yesterday I had torn up a news story and photo: the lovely Miss So-and-So spent the evening in such-and-such a nightclub. The young man sitting with her spilled his drink on her dress and she emptied a bottle on his suit. I said, that must have cost at least a hundred pounds. I said, at that price ...

But all this is beside the point.

Going on, he said to me: 'We'll put them in cardboard boxes and find trucks to bring them free of charge. We'll distribute them sealed and that way it will be a surprise.' A surprise. War is surprise too. That's what the Chinese writer Sun Tsi said five hundred years before Christ. I was half asleep and I couldn't control this folly. Such accidents occasionally happen to me, especially when I'm tired, and then I can't believe my eyes. I look at people and ask: are these really our faces? All this mud that June has vomited on to them, how could we have cleaned it off so quickly? Can we really be smiling? Is it true? ...

But this, too, is beside the point.

As the telephone receiver slipped from my hand, he said: 'On the morning of the holiday, every child will get a sealed package, with a surprise toy inside it. It will be luck.' The receiver fell. The pillow carried me back nineteen years.

It was the year 1949.

They told us that day: the Red Cross will bring all you children presents for the holiday. I was wearing short pants and a grey cotton shirt and open shoes without socks. The winter was the worst the region had ever seen and when I set out that morning my fingers froze and were covered with something like fine glass. I sat down on the pavement and began to cry. Then a man came by and carried me to a nearby shop where they were lighting a wood fire in some kind of tin container. They brought me close and I stretched my feet towards the flame. Then I went racing to the Red Cross Centre, and stood with the hundreds of children, all of us waiting for our turn.

The boxes seemed very far away and we were trembling like a field of sugar cane and hopping about in order to keep the blood flowing in our veins. After a million years, my turn came.

A clean starched nurse gave me a red square box.

I ran 'home' without opening it. Now, nineteen years later, I have completely forgotten what was in that dream box. Except for just one thing: a can of lentil soup.

I clutched the soup can with my two hands red from the cold and pressed it to my chest in front of ten other children, my brothers and relatives, who looked at it with their twenty wide eyes.

Probably the box held splendid children's toys too, but these weren't to eat and so I didn't pay any attention to them and they got lost. I kept the can of soup for a week, and every day I gave my mother some of it in a water glass so she could cook it for us.

I remember nothing except the cold, and the ice that manacled my fingers, and the can of soup.

The voice of the man who wakes up early was still ringing in my head that tired grey morning when the bells began to clang in a dreadful emptiness. I returned from my trip into the past which continued to throb in my head, and ...

But all of that too is beside the point.

Translated by Barbara Harlow

ABDELRAHIM MAHMOUD

The Martyr

My soul I shall carry on my palm
and throw it into the valley of death

For it is either a life that pleases a friend
or a death that the enemy it shall infuriate

Two aims the nobleman's soul has
Approaching fate and reaching destiny

What is life for if dreaded not is
my presence, and inviolability is my fame

If I speak the world listens
and my speech's echo resounding it is

My martyrdom I see coming
but towards it my pace I mend

The rattling of swords my ear enjoys
and the spilling of my blood shall thrill my soul

Over the hills his body is braided
And the sky's predators skirmish on

A share for lions of the sky there is
and a share for the cats of evil
With purple his blood the soil it attired
and the wind of youth it perfumed

Soiled the charm of the forehead it did
but a soiling is that beauty it increases

On his lips a smile showed
meaning ridicule for this world it is
Dreamt of eternal life and slept to dream
it to enjoy the best of perceives
I seek death rather than lose my rights
and my country it is the goal

Men's death that is what it is for
and who wants a noble death this is what it is

Fear I don't ... and for me life is cheap in disgrace
when the symbol of disdain is that what I am

With my heart the face of the enemy I shall slap
for my heart is steel and my fire inflames

My homeland with the edge of the sword I shall protect
and my people shall know I am the man for it

Translated by Adib S. Kawar

The Aqsa Mosque

Honourable Prince! Before you stands a poet
whose heart harbours bitter complaint.
Have you come to visit the Aqsa mosque
or to bid it farewell before it is lost?
This land, this holy land, is being sold to all intruders
and stabbed by its own people!
And tomorrow looms over us, nearer and nearer!
Nothing shall remain for us but our streaming tears,
our deep regrets!
Oh, Prince, shout, shout! Your voice
might shake people awake!
Ask the guards of the Aqsa: are they all agreed to struggle
as one body and mind?

Translated by Salma K. Jayyusi and Trevor LeGassick

ABDELKARIM AL-KARMI

We Will Return

Beloved Palestine, how do I sleep
While the spectrum of torture is in my eyes
I purify the world with your name
And if your love did not tire me out,
I would've kept my feelings a secret
The caravans of days pass and talk about
The conspiracy of enemies and friends
Beloved Palestine! How do I live
Away from your plains and mounds?
The feet of mountains that are dyed with blood
Are calling me
And on the horizon appears the dye
The weeping shores are calling me
And my weeping echoes in the ears of time
The escaping streams are calling me
They are becoming foreign in their land
Your orphan cities are calling me
And your villages and domes
My friends ask me, 'Will we meet again?'
'Will we return?'
Yes! We will kiss the bedewed soil
And the red desires are on our lips
Tomorrow, we will return
And the generations will hear

The sound of our footsteps
We will return along with the storms
Along with the lightning and meteors
Along with the hope and songs
Along with the flying eagle
Along with the dawn that smiles to the deserts
Along with the morning on the waves of the sea
Along with the bleeding flags
And along with the shining swords and spears

Translated by Sharif S. Elmusa and Naomi Shihab Nye

SAMIRA AZZAM

Man and His Alarm Clock

It's not quite four AM. I woke up twenty minutes before the alarm. Why don't I simply say that I didn't know the taste of sleep that night? The thought that I would work tomorrow was excitement itself. Before I turned in, I stood at length before the only two suits I owned. I had to choose one to wear for my first day at work. I preferred the grey suit but my mother said, 'You wore it to your interview with the manager. Wear the other.' How do women remember such details? I had of course forgotten. I set my little alarm clock to ring at four AM, but I woke up three times, anxious that it would let me down, and tested it every time. When I was instructing my mother to wake me, my aunt volunteered. So did my sister and father. Really, I didn't sleep a wink that night. When the alarm clock jingled loudly I jumped out of bed. My mother, my aunt, and my sister all jumped too, my mother to heat up water for me to shave and wash, my aunt to prepare for me a generous breakfast the likes of which I had never seen before (after all I was employed now), and my sister to shine my shoes. I was standing in the bathroom, massaging shaving cream on my face, and whistling some kind of a tune to cover my nervousness, when we heard the sound of slow but deliberate knocking. My aunt rushed to the front door. She stopped short when she remembered that most people would not yet have started their day. I raced to the door behind her but once I arrived I too hesitated. I collected myself then asked, 'Who is it?' From behind the two adjoining leaves of our door, I heard someone say, 'Are you awake, Mr. Fathi?'

I put my hand on the doorknob and turned it. By the time it opened the night caller had already turned around and I could only make out a vague shape moving away in the dark. In wonder, I went back to shaving. My aunt did not waste the chance to brag. She said in no uncertain terms, 'Fathi's job must be really important! Otherwise why would the government bother to wake him up?' I savoured my aunt's explanation without hesitation, and proudly. I basked in my new sense of self-importance as I got dressed, wolfed down two eggs, reprimanded my sister when she whispered unwanted advice in my ear, wrapped my coat around me, and made for the door, with my aunt's prayers blowing through the cracks of the front door and slapping my back until the dawn call to prayer finally drowned them out. Her voice faded into that of the muezzin, waves of sound which arose from his very depths only to melt into the white light of dawn and settle on the ears of people on the street, like familiar, soft dew, coaxing smiles on their faces, relaxing muscles tensed in the stinging wind.

Prayer is better than sleep. But my village was asleep. For the first time in my life I could hear the noise my shoes made on the pavement as I prompted my feet to catch up with the boy who worked at the bakery, and whose head and neck seemed to have disappeared into a fantastic felt hat.

The train station was on the other side of town. There had been an upheaval when it was built, a structure quite at odds with the city's historical walls, about two kilometres away from the southern gate. To reach the gate we have to go through an old market, a hub of buzzing activity during the day with people selling and buying grains and whatever else can be weighed on scales. Traders, brokers, and beasts of burden mill around, while the donkey sticks its snout into any open bag of grain as it waits for its master to conclude his bargain with one trader or another.

It was, however, silent, empty of any pedestrian, and desolate when I went by at dawn. I almost broke into a run but quickly held myself back when I remembered that I was now an employee. I walked energetically across the market, passed through the southern gate and traversed the distance between the gate and the station. I boarded the train displaying the pass my new employer had provided me. It might have attracted the attention of two young men sitting across from me but they did not try to pry. I didn't dare speak to them either. I occupied myself with watching the distances folding up quickly before my eyes, fixed on a horizon now, as morning arrived, aglitter with the colours of dawn.

My first day at work was no easy affair. There were those looks, inspecting, questioning, snubbing, disparaging ... There were those enigmatic files, those numbers without beginning or end, and those codes that required instant breaking. It took no time for my pride to dwindle. I was nothing but a tiny unknown speck in a mighty institution crowded with giants. If my aunt could see me at work she would have revised her opinion of me and thought the two eggs I devoured earlier in the morning were too good for me. I had presumed – given that someone was sent to wake me – that I was important. My first day at work taught me that I was but a timid cat frightened by a fierce dog.

I was eating two eggs again the following morning, however, when the same voice came to wake me. The wake-up call did really make me feel important. In fact, I did not even mind opening the door and muttering whatever words of thanks I could think of at the time. We often derive pleasure from the justifications we make and rarely question them. My aunt succeeded in convincing me of its importance for a whole month, for as long as the night caller came to wake me every dawn. I even stopped opening the door to greet my caller.

I was more than surprised when I heard a colleague say, after I managed finally, following ten months of trying, to melt a mountain of ice that the old timers erected before their new colleagues, that the knocks of Abu Fuad were more accurate than any clock, and without them he would have had to take a taxi to work every day to get to his job in Haifa. He would definitely have missed his train if he had relied only on his alarm clock.

It then dawned on me that my night visitor could be a real person, who had a name, a personality, distinct features, and maybe even a life lived in particular circumstances. Until then he had only been a voice I heard repeating the same phrase every dawn. And now that I discovered, by accident, that he had a name, I thought he must have a face too.

When I heard him knock on our door the following day, I opened it faster than he could walk away. When he saw me he responded to my greetings with little enthusiasm, 'You are Fathi?' He was a middle-aged man whose body seemed to disappear into his black coat and an old dark fez. But his posture gave the impression that he was always ready to give the door in front of him a knock, on the dot, without fail. I felt obliged to invite him in, please, come in, but he excused himself. He said he had to wake Ghassan, Abdallah, Yusuf, and, and, and ... He turned around, left me, and was immediately swallowed by darkness. I asked my new friend Abdallah about him when we were travelling to work on the same train, trying to picture him as a person. The heart-breaking story I heard was not new to me.

We live in a very small village and our stories are not secrets. The kind villagers were all saddened one evening – just as my mother, my aunt, my sister, and the neighbours visiting that night had been – when they heard the tragic story of Fuad. Fuad was an employee at the railway company. He arrived late one morning and the train had already started to pull out of the station.

He jumped, hung on to one of the doors and tried to get on, but his hands failed him. He slipped and he fell on the tracks. Tender youth turned into an unrecognisable lump of flesh under the train's heartless wheels.

During that week the village had mourned the young man, repeating to each other the drama of flesh meeting steel. We learned that his father was a thread merchant who owned a small shop in the cloth market. His wares did not exceed a few plaits of thread in a variety of colours hanging on the walls and a scale that caught my eye for its diminutive size. I saw these when my aunt sent me there to buy her two-dirham worth of yellow silk thread she would use to mend the rims of a scarf she loved to wear. The accident happened two years ago. When I remembered all the details I forgot to ask my friend about the relationship between the accident and the task Fuad's father had taken upon himself to awaken all the employees of the company. I could not suppress my curiosity until the evening. I left my office to look for Abdallah and find out from him. By the time I returned I was even sadder than when I heard about Fuad's horrific death that evening two years before. The father, who had lost his only son, took it upon himself to get up before dawn, make his rounds in the village, and wake all his son's colleagues, one by one, so that no one would be late, and as a result meet a similar fate as his son.

I brought the story home with me and told my family at our dinner table, not concerned about diminishing my own importance in front of them as I revealed the identity of my night caller. My mother wept. My aunt knitted her brows without shedding a tear or a pause in her chewing. However, she made a tremendous effort to be kind the next morning. She got up early, this after she had stopped getting up to prepare my breakfast a week after I began going to work, rushing to the door to open it as soon as she heard a knock. She even brought the coffee pot and a cup with her, and then swore an oath insisting that the poor man drink a cup of coffee even as he stood by the door.

That happened a week before the harsh winter morning when things took another horrific turn. It had rained so hard that the sewers flooded and water was running everywhere, washing the paved alleyways and filling the furrows time had ploughed between one tile and another. I had not set my alarm clock. I had stopped doing that when I knew for sure that my night caller was as accurate if not more. I was lingering in my bed, snuggled up under my warm blanket like a cat curled up in front of a heater, postponing the moment I would get up until I heard the knock on our door. As soon as I heard it, I threw my blanket off me, not bothering to look at the clock, got dressed, and gobbled up my breakfast. When I opened the door, a man huddled against the door took me by surprise. It was as if he was trying to avoid the light drizzle and the raindrops bouncing off the roof's edge.

As I went out the door, I said to him, 'A rainy morning, isn't it?', to which he replied, as if apologising for standing there, 'I'm not lingering here because of the rain. The truth is that I was late. I overslept. Maybe the rain delayed me too. Today I started by waking your colleagues first and came to you last. Run, my son, for you only have ten minutes to make it to the station'.

I still took time to look at my watch under the street lamp covered in raindrops. Only nine minutes to departure time, hardly enough for me to make it to the southern gate. I pulled myself together and walked as fast as my strength would allow me, doubling my usual speed, until I made it to the paved alleys of the covered market. Every time I stopped to catch my breath, I saw before my eyes a bloody lump of flesh that had been a human being with two good feet, just like me, before the wheels minced him, hurrying to make it to his job at the railway company. I could taste tragedy in my mouth but could also feel strange power in my feet.

I reached the train before it moved. I was even able to get on and take my usual place, though breathless. It would have been all right for the train to move after I had arrived, as long as I did not have to hang onto its door and fall beneath its wheels. But the train did not move. We understood that a minor fault requiring a few minutes for repair had delayed the train's departure. The train always ran on schedule, like clockwork. Out of the open window I saw the fields soaking up the rain and the tall grass bending under the weight of the heavy drops. The station that never sleeps was packed with porters who, having finished loading luggage or merchandise, were now sitting on the kerb drinking tea and spitting. I was looking intently at the pastry and egg seller when I saw the night caller who, on the other side of the door, looked to me as if he were wiping his face, brushing water off his wet fez, and catching his breath with difficulty.

What brought him to the station? Would he be travelling today as well? Was he afraid that I would miss my train and came after me to make sure I made it? I did not have any definitive answers, for the hoarse whistle of the train tore into the grey lights of dawn, the wheels screeched on the tracks, the noise of their movement surged, and the train lurched forward. As the train moved farther and farther away from the station I could no longer see him except as a dark dot against the horizon, without any distinct features.

When I heard the knock on the door the following dawn all the details of the morning before came back to me. I was relieved to know that the man did not get hurt while chasing me to the station in the pouring rain. I did not link his earlier exhaustion to his absence from our door two days later. I thought his knocks were drowned out by the cranking noise the gas stove made in our old kitchen. I only knew for certain when I heard Abdallah wondering about the reason for his absence.

He did not come the day after, or the third. Our curiosity and astonishment kept us talking all the way home from work in the afternoon. My colleagues charged me with the task of inquiring after him at his little shop in the cloth market. I decided to go to the shop before I went home. I had to ask about its exact location twice. When I finally reached it I found its door closed but the sign still intact in its usual place. I asked his neighbour who said, 'He is either away or sick. He is a man of few words and we are not nosy. If there is anything you want from his shop, we have the same and better merchandise.'

I took the news to Abdallah and we decided to look for his house the next day. We really missed him. I was the most anxious of them all, for I was so afraid that I was the cause of his indisposition. We set out in the morning to look for his house, and after inquiring with his neighbours, we arrived at a wooden door behind which, as we understood, was a courtyard that would lead us to the two rooms in which the man lived. We had already asked two boys in the street whether they had seen the man that day and they said no. Abdallah was about to turn around, for he preferred to make it to his daily journey, but I was not satisfied. I could not explain why, but a hunch drove me to work the outer door, which opened easily to my touch. A courtyard unfurled before our eyes. Half of it was paved with tiles, and a small fountain stood on the unpaved half, as well as naked oleanders. I saw another door in front of me. One of the two hinges had come off. I knocked on the door. Silence replied. I knocked a second time. Abdallah joined me this time. Our knocks drew out a woman next door. She looked out from a window above the courtyard and watched us curiously. We knocked again. While feeling the doorknob, Abdallah said, 'We'd better go,' but I refused. I felt an unknown misgiving and a pricking pain in my conscience. I put my hand on the doorknob once more and tried turning it again but when the door would not open I put my weight against it and pushed hard. I knew the door had opened when I almost fell. I went in. Abdallah stayed behind and stood by the outer door waiting for me. He did not want to have anything to do with this intrusion.

I went into the first room. In the middle was a table with breadcrumbs and the remains of a meal on top. There was another room behind it. It had two black iron beds. I thought the one that was carefully made must have been the dead young man's bed. I saw on the other bed blankets piled on top of something. I pulled myself together and tried to get close to it but my courage failed me when I saw an open mouth and two glassy eyes.

The man was dead, like everything else in the room, the small dark chest, the desk beneath a striped tablecloth, and the mirror marked by yellow dots as if it were a reflection of an ugly face. Nothing was alive in the room except the clock mounted on the wall, its timepiece swaying in a dance, and singing a tick tock tune.

Translated by Wen-Chin Ouyang, Michael Beard and Nora E. Parr

JABRA IBRAHIM JABRA

Hunters in a Narrow Street

When you arrive in a big city you are so excited that you do not deliberate too long about what hotel to stay in, because the streets are crying out to have you walk in them, and you feel an air of expectation about the city as if all these years it had been decking itself out for your benefit. You want to rush out and see it all in an hour; and within that hour are compressed the adventures of your dreams. Nothing is so exhilarating as the sight of unknown buildings and unfamiliar faces, after the eagerness that has worked up in you during the long journey and the longer preparations before it. And was Baghdad a big city? I had asked someone in Damascus. 'It certainly is,' came the answer. 'There are fourteen cabarets in it.'

I, however, on the first day of October, 1948, felt little exhilaration and less excitement on my arrival. It was not because I had seen London and Paris and Cairo and Damascus. I had forgotten my travels and could not remember what any city in the world looked like – any city, except one. Only one city did I remember, and remember all the time. I had left a part of my life buried under its rubble, under its gutted trees and fallen roofs, and I came to Baghdad with my eyes still lingering on it – Jerusalem.

Some eighteen months before, we had moved into our recently built house on the Katamon hill in New Jerusalem. The house was the fulfilment of my father's dream, and the result of a lifetime of toil and saving. On my return from England after World War II, I had chosen the spot myself on an eminence which on one side bordered on the hills of the country, and on the other on the beautiful road that wound its way to the heart of the city. But it also overlooked the Jewish quarter of Rehavia, whence I often saw from the balcony odd couples coming up and ringing our bell. They were attracted by the arched entrance, they said; by the geraniums on the white-stone staircase; and by the three-pillared tall windows on the second floor which, catching the sun, rose like a flame over the valley. 'Do you let rooms?' they asked. Sometimes we offered them coffee and they commented on my furniture and books, and left effusive with admiration for the 'Arab way of life'.

Next door to us lived the Shahins in a house twice as big as ours. They were a patriarchal family: the grandparents, the parents and the children made the house noisy and suggestive of tribal happiness, on which my brother and I commented freely in our quiet rooms. But hardly had two months passed before Leila Shahin, the eldest of the children, and I took eager notice of each other. The first few times we met we were as secretive about it as we could be. We walked about the rocky unbuilt-up part of the hill in the dark, often defying the mad barking of stray dogs, until I said, 'Look here, Leila, I love you, and I can't keep it secret any longer.'

She had long chestnut hair always rather untidy, brown eyes, a large mouth and fair skin. We went for long drives in my small Morris, and were careful not to be seen by too many people. Two or three times I took her to a Jewish café in Rehavia where we could dance. Much to my surprise one evening her mother called on us, introduced herself and had a long chat with my mother. I understood. When she left I told mother about Leila and she said, 'Isn't it shameful of you both to have an affair behind our backs? Is that what you learned at Cambridge?'

'But I love her,' I said.

'I will not hear such shameful talk. If you love her, do something about it. But remember, having just built this expensive house we've got no money left for a wedding just now. Besides, your father has been only eight months dead.'

After that Leila and I met openly and our families exchanged visits. More often however we met when they could not see us, until Leila once said, 'Will you ever kiss me enough? It's terrifying.' And I said, 'I want you like mad. We must get married soon. Will you come and live with us?' 'Yes, Yes, Yes,' she said jubilantly. 'It's like going to the neighbours and not coming back ever after, isn't it?'

Some nights later we were woken up by a succession of violent explosions that rocked our house. Jewish terrorists had been killing the British for several years, blowing up government offices, army barracks, officers' clubs. Now they had started on the Arabs. United Nations had recommended splitting Palestine in two, and the terrorists were determined to achieve the bloody dichotomy. Barrels of TNT were set off in market squares, killing about fifty people at a time, and now it was the beautiful white and rose stone houses of the Arabs they were after. When we went out, trembling with fear, to see what had happened, we saw three great heaps, about three hundred yards away, smoking into the cold air of early dawn. Some British soldiers were soon there to investigate the rubble.

Our quarter, being on the fringe, was in the grip of terror. Three or four people produced revolvers with which they said they would defend their homes. A villager offered me a rifle, an old German Mauser, with exactly five rounds. My brother bought it on the spot, but neither he nor I had ever fired a shot in our lives. The villager showed us how to fire, but we could not spare a single bullet for a live try.

That night we did not sleep. The terrorists did not come. Three nights later there was a mad howling storm. It thundered and rumbled and rain fell ferociously for hours. The power suddenly failed, and the whole quarter was in foul darkness. Every now and then the lightning gave us a glimpse of the hills through the uncurtained windows. The rifle stood on its butt in the corner.

Nothing could be heard but storm and thunder. And we dozed off, dressed in our overcoats. It was December. Then there was a blinding flash, and the house shook as in an earthquake, and the glass was blown in, crashing on the floor. I was stunned. My mother screamed. Yacoub dashed to the rifle in the corner and through the now paneless window tried to fire – at nothing that he could see, but he thought he had heard a car shooting off at the same time as the explosion. But no fire came out and he pulled the trigger again. The rifle might have been a toy. It jammed.

When I looked out, I cried in horror. The Shahins' house was a great heap of masonry, faintly perceptible through the black night. We ran downstairs and out into the howling wind. What could we do? In a few minutes other people came. We started turning the stones over to see if there was any life trapped underneath. 'God, keep Leila alive, keep Leila alive,' I was saying to myself, and like a madman I skipped about the rubble and the great stones and the iron girders in vain hope. Then I felt something soft hit my hand. I dug it up. It was a hand torn off the wrist. It was Leila's hand, with the engagement ring buckled round the third finger. I sat down and cried.

During the next day the engineers of the British army unearthed eleven corpses piecemeal. Leila's hand was returned to her battered body. One funeral was enough for the collective family burial. What was I to do to the faceless anonymous enemy? In our impotence, unarmed and defenceless, we vowed revenge. But the quarter on the hill was open and exposed to the nocturnal terror, like a helpless supine woman. In twenty-four hours it was evacuated. We found a two-room house in nearby Bethlehem. We had not spent three nights in our new refuge when our house, pillars and all, was turned into another large weird mass of ruins. Yacoub and I went to see the iron girders sticking out of the wreckage and pointing twisted fingers to a cold blue sky. The ruins of blown-up houses stood in a row, as in a nightmare.

Jerusalem was an embattled city. The most unorganised, the most unarmed collection of volunteers, trying to stop the fanning out of a highly organised, well-armed and ruthless force: a few erratic bullets against mines of gelignite. Soon the British army left the fighters to their fate, and hell set into the vacuum on its trail. We were cut off from Jerusalem and the Arabs of the city took shelter behind the great Ottoman walls, where their rifles could keep off the armoured cars of the Jewish Skull Squadrons. Night and day were filled with gun-fire.

Arab villagers were massacred in the treacherous dark by men they had never seen, and nothing saved our town of Christ except the desperate volunteers who entrenched themselves in the hills and declivities around the town, and grimly waited and sniped and forayed and retired. We all bought our own rifles (I had to buy another one) despite the exorbitant prices (who knowns what group trafficked with those rusty outmoded weapons and came out with fearful profits?), and we would take our positions in what we considered strategic points, to keep the enemy off until the Arab Legion came to the rescue. On clear nights, we went down the terraces of the valley of Bethlehem; I could not help wondering what diabolical irony made of such a lovely place, thick with olive trees, the scene of our ill-equipped defiance of hate. Where the angels had appeared to the shepherds two thousand years ago to sing of joy and peace to men, we daily faced the ever-spluttering messengers of death.

And time dragged and sorrow came upon sorrow without relief. Despite all our fears we had preserved a little hope, but each new day ate further into our hope. It was a war, we were told. It was the greatest practical joke in the world, and the most tragic one. There were armies; there were guns; there were generals; there were strategists; there were mediators. But the dislodged and the dispossessed multiplied. There was a truce, yet the refugees came in greater numbers. They carried their rags and their bundles, and buried their children unceremoniously under the olive trees. Amidst the wild flowers rest the torn pieces of flesh, human and animal inextricably twined. In the spacious courtyard of the Byzantine Church of Christ's Nativity slept a tangled tattered mass of peasants and mules and camels, and only the braying of asses was louder than the hungry crying of children.

In the town square an enterprising café proprietor had installed a battery of radio with a loudspeaker. Wireless sets were becoming cumbersome pieces of furniture since the cutting off of power in New Jerusalem. So the people would congregate in thousands in the town square to hear the news on the small café radio, three times a day, at eight, at two, at six, and when the hour was announced by the broadcasting station with its usual six pips, a hush would fall upon the listening crowd, all eager for one item of good news. Every day at the appointed hours the thousands gathered in hope and fifteen minutes later dispersed in agony. 'When Jerusalem is open again ...' that was the phrase on every tongue. 'When Jerusalem is open again ...' They would climb up the mountain of Beit Jala to have a look at the city they loved spreading the northern horizon in a haze of pale violet, no more than six miles away, but as good as a hundred thousand miles away, a city of dreams looming beyond a valley of death.

In the Deserts of Exile

Spring after spring,
In the deserts of exile,
What are we doing with our love,
When our eyes are full of frost and dust?
Our Palestine, green land of ours;
Its flowers as if embroidered of women's gowns;
March adorns its hills
With the jewel-like peony and narcissus;
April bursts open in its plains
With flowers and bride-like blossoms;
May is our rustic song
Which we sing at noon,
In the blue shadows,
Among the olive trees of our valley
And in the ripeness of the fields
We wait for the promise of July
And the joyous dance amidst the harvest.
O land of ours where our childhood passed
Like dreams in the shade of the orange-grove,
Among the almond-trees in the valleys –
Remember us now wandering
Among the thorns of the desert,
Wandering in rocky mountains;
Remember us now
In the tumult of cities beyond deserts and seas;
Remember us
With our eyes full of dust
That never clears in our ceaseless wandering.
They crushed the flowers on the hills around us,
Destroyed the houses over our heads,

Scattered our torn remains,
Then unfolded the desert before us,
With valleys writhing in hunger
And blue shadows shattered into red thorns
Bent over corpses left as prey for falcon and crow.
Is it from your hills that the angels sang to the shepherds
Of peace on earth and goodwill among men?
Only death laughed when it saw
Among the entrails of beasts
The ribs of men,
And through the guffaw of bullets
It went dancing a joyous dance
On the heads of weeping women.
Our land is an emerald,
But in the deserts of exile,
Spring after spring,
Only the dust hisses in our face.
What then, what are we doing with our love?
When our eyes and our mouth are full of frost and dust?

Translated by Mounah Khouri and Hamid Algar

EMILE HABIBI

Excerpt from The Secret Life of Saeed, The Pessoptimist

I found that we were then at a crossroad between Nazareth and Nahlal, passing the plain of Ibn Amir. The big man signalled to the policemen through the glass window separating him from 'the dogs'. They led me out and stuffed me in between the big man and the driver. I made myself comfortable and sighed, breathed the fresh air deep, and remarked, 'Oh, I see we're in the plain of Ibn Amir.' Obviously annoyed, he corrected me: 'No, it's the Yizrael plain.'

'What's in a name?', as Shakespeare put it, I soothed him. I spoke the line in English, causing him to murmur, 'Oh, so you quote Shakespeare, do you?'

***

As we descended further down into the plain toward its city of Affulah, with the hills of Nazareth to our left, the big man began reciting to me the principles governing my new life in prison, the etiquette of behaviour toward the jailers who were my superiors and the other inmates who were my inferiors. He promised, moreover, to get me promoted to a liaison position. While he was going through these lessons, I became ever more certain that what is required of us inside prison is no different from what is required from us on the outside. My delight at this discovery was so great that I exclaimed joyfully, 'Why, God bless you, sir!'

He went on: 'If a jailer should call you, your first response must be: Yes, sir! And if he should tell you off, you must reply: At your command, sir! And if you should hear from your fellow inmates engaging in any conversation that threatens the security of the prison, even by implication, you must inform the warden. Now, if he should give you a beating, then say—' I interrupted him with a proper response, 'That's your right, sir!'

'How did you know that? Were you ever imprisoned before?'

'Oh, no. God forbid, sir, that anyone should have beaten you to this favour! I have merely noticed according to your account of prison rules of etiquette and behaviour that your prison treats inmates with great humanitarianism and compassion – just as you treat us on the outside. And we behave the same, too. But how do you punish Arabs who are criminals, sir?'

'This bothers us considerably. That's why our minister general has said that our occupation has been the most compassionate on Earth ever since Paradise was liberated from its Occupation of Adam and Eve. Among our leadership there are some who believe that we treat Arabs inside prisons even better than we treat them outside, though this latter treatment is, as you know, excellent. These same leaders are convinced that we thus encourage them to continue to resist our civilisational mission in the new territories, just like those ungrateful African cannibals who eat their benefactors.'

'How do you mean, sir?'

'Well, take for example our policy of punishing people with exile. This we award them without their going to jail. If they once entered jail, they would become as firmly established there as British occupation once was. '

'Yes, God bless you indeed, sir!'

'And we demolish their homes when they're outside, but when they're inside prison we let them occupy themselves building.'

'That's really great! God bless you! But what do they build?'

'New prisons and new cells in old jails: and they plant shade trees around them too.'

'God bless you again! But why do you demolish their homes outside the prison?'

'To exterminate the rats that build their nests in them. This way we save them from the plague.'

* * *

By now the police car was leaving the city of Affulah on the Bisan road, which led to my new residence. On both sides refreshing water was being sprayed on the green vegetation, fresh in the very heat of summer. Suddenly the big man, cramped there with me and the driver in the front seat of that dogcart, was transformed into a poet.

While I sat there being my usual Pessoptimistic self, he was ecstatic: 'Verdant fields! Green on your right and on your left: green everywhere! We have given life to what was dead. This is why we have named the borders of Israel the Green Belt. For beyond them lie barren mountains and desert reaches, a wilderness calling out to us, 'Come ye hither, tractors of civilization!'

* * *

I looked before me and saw a huge building towering like an ugly demon of the desert; its walls were yellow, and around it there was a high, white outer wall. There were guards posted on each of the four sides of the roof, and they could be seen standing with their guns at the ready. We were awestruck by the spectacle of this yellow castle, so exposed and naked of any vegetation, protruding like a cancerous lump on the breast of a land itself sick with cancer.

The big man was unable to control himself and exclaimed, 'There! The terrible Shatta prison! How fantastic!'

I stretched my neck forward in alarm and whispered, 'God bless us all!'

This led him to comment, 'It is the prison warden who will bless you. Come on down. I'll ask him to look after you.'

Translated by Salma K. Jayyusi and Trevor LeGassick

EDWARD SAID

On Edward Said's Experience of the Nakba

Not to hold back my conclusion, which is roughly the same as Noam (Chomsky)'s, I want to say also that my feeling is that the two-state solution for the Palestinian-Israeli conflict is, I think, a hopeless one, and some form of bi-nationalism, which I'll try to get to at the end of my comments, seems to me to be the only hope, and hence the reason for talking about it more in this country. I've just come back a couple of weeks ago from a trip where I spent some time in Israel, as well as, of course, in the Palestinian territories, and spoke about this to some degree of response from Israelis – I mean, Israeli Jews – and, of course, Israeli Palestinians.

But what I want to do today is to talk a little bit about the importance, the continuing importance, of 1948 for the present moment. And in a sense, I want to talk about something quite different than what you've heard from Noam Chomsky. That is to say, I want to talk about the Palestinian experience as a human – evolving human thing, trajectory, and how it feeds into the current impasse and where it might, if looked at honestly within the Arab and international context, might give one some hope for the future, which I think is the most important thing.

I might as well begin by speaking personally about 1948, particularly at a moment when the media is focusing so much on the faces and the bodies and general appalling plight of Kosovar refugees, and what it meant for many of the people around me. My own immediate family was spared the worst ravages of what we call the catastrophe, or Nakba, of 1948. We had a house and my father, a business in Cairo, so even though we were in Palestine during most of 1947, when we left in December of that year, the wrenching cataclysmic quality of the collective experience, when 780,000 Palestinians – two-thirds of the population – were literally driven out of the country by the Zionist forces of the time, this was not one we had to go through in as traumatic a form as most others did.

I was twelve at the time, so I had only a somewhat attenuated and certainly no more than a semi-conscious awareness of what was happening. Only this narrow awareness was available to me, but I do distinctly recall some things with special lucidity. One was that every member of my family, on both sides, became a refugee during the period. No one remained in our Palestine, that is, that part of the mandatory territory controlled by the British Mandate. That didn't include the West Bank, which was in 1948 annexed to Jordan. Therefore, those of my relatives who lived in cities like Jaffa, Safed, Haifa and West Jerusalem, which is where I was born, were suddenly made homeless, in many instances – penniless, disoriented and scarred forever.

I saw most of them again after the fall of Palestine, but all were greatly reduced in circumstances – their faces stark with worry, ill health, despair. My extended family lost all its property and residence, and like so many Palestinians of the time, bore the travail not so much as a political, but as a natural tragedy. This etched itself on my memory with lasting results, mostly because of the faces which I had once remembered as content and at ease, but which now were lined with the cares of exile and homelessness, which is the condition of most Palestinians today. Many families and individuals had their lives broken, their spirits drained, their composure destroyed forever in the context of seemingly unending serial dislocation. This was, and still is, for me of the greatest poignancy. One of my uncles went from Palestine to Alexandria, to Cairo, to Baghdad, to Beirut, and now, in his eighties, lives a sad, silent man in Seattle. Neither he nor his immediate family ever truly recovered.

This is emblematic of the larger story of loss and dispossession which continues today. And I think it ought to be mentioned that ever since 1948, the United Nations – just as NATO is saying today and the United States along with it – ever since 1948, the United States with the United Nations has voted a yearly resolution saying that the Palestinians can go back.

The second thing I recall was that, for the one person in my family who somehow managed to pull herself together in the aftermath of the catastrophe, my aunt, Palestine meant service to the unfortunate refugees, many thousands of whom ended up penniless, jobless, destitute and disoriented in Egypt. She devoted her life to them in the face of government obduracy and sadistic indifference. From her, I learned that whereas everyone is willing to pay lip service to the cause, to the humanitarian cause, only a very few people were willing to do anything about it. As a Palestinian, therefore, she took it as her lifelong duty to set about helping the refugees. This was in the days before UNICEF and USAID and all of those other things, getting people and children into schools, getting them doctors, getting them treatment and medicine, finding the men jobs, and so on and so forth. She remains an exemplary figure for me, a person against whom any effort thereafter is always measured and always found wanting. The job for us in my lifetime was to be literally unending. It's now fifty-one years. And because it derives from a human tragedy so profound, so extraordinary and saturating, both the formal as well as the informal life of its people, down to the smallest detail has been and will continue to be recalled, testified, remedied. For Palestinians, a vast collective feeling of injustice continues to hang over our lives with undiminished weight.

If there's been one thing, one particular delinquency committed by the present group of Palestinian leaders for me, it is their gifted power of forgetting. When one of them was asked recently – this appeared on the front page of the *New York Times* last October – what he felt about Ariel Sharon's accession to Israel's foreign ministry, given that Sharon was responsible for the shedding of so much Palestinian blood, this leader said blithely, 'We are prepared to forget history.' And this is a sentiment I neither can share nor, I hasten to add, easily forgive.

It's therefore important to recall what Israelis themselves have said about the country they conquered in 1948. Here's Moshe Dayan, 1969, April, just about thirty years ago today: 'We came to this country which was already populated by Arabs, and we are establishing a Hebrew, that is a Jewish state here. In considerable areas of the country' – the total area of the country that he's talking about was only 6 percent – 'we bought the lands from the Arabs. Jewish villages were built in the place of Arab villages. You do not even know' – he was talking to an Israeli audience. 'You do not even know the names of these Arab villages, and I do not blame you, because these geography books no longer exist; not only do the books not exist, the Arab villages are not there either.' In the events of 1948, 400 villages were destroyed and effaced from history. 'Nahalal,' which is Dayan's own village, he says, 'arose in the place of Mahalul, Gevat – in the place of Jibta, [Kibbutz] Sarid – in the place of Haneifs and Kefar Yehoshua – in the place of Tell Shaman. There is not' – this is the last sentence of his intervention – 'There is not one place built in this country that did not have a former Arab population.'

Looking back on the reactions in the aftermath of 1948, what strikes me now is how largely unpolitical they were, as it must be the case for people going through what some of the refugees are going through today. For twenty years after 1948, Palestinians were immersed in the problems of everyday life, with little time left over for organising, analysing and planning. Israel, to most Arabs, for at least twenty years after '48, and to Palestinians, except for those who remained, was a cipher: its language unknown, its society unexplored, its people and the history and their movement largely confined to slogans, catch-all phrases, negation. We saw and experienced its cruelty towards us, but it took us a long while to understand what we saw and what we experienced. The overall tendency throughout the Arab world – and this is one of the most important consequences of 1948, as I'm sure it will be in regions of the world that are going through the same process today – is that a vast militarisation took over every society, almost without exception, as it did also take over Israel. Coup in the Arab world, military coups, succeeded each other more or less unceasingly. And worse yet, every advance in the military idea brought an equal and opposite diminution in social, political and economic democracy.

Looking back on it now, the rise to hegemony of Arabic nationalism allowed for very little in the way of democratic civil institutions, mainly because the concepts and the language of that nationalism devoted little attention to the role of democracy in the evolution of these societies. Until now, the presence of a putative danger to the Arab world has engendered a permanent deferral of such things as an open press, unpoliticised universities, or freedoms to research, travel in and explore new realms of knowledge. No massive investment was ever made in the quality of education despite, on the whole, successful policies by some governments, including the Egyptian government, to lower the rate of illiteracy. It was thought that given the perpetual state of emergency caused by Israel, such matters, which could only be the result of long-range planning and reflection, were luxuries that were ill-afforded. Instead, arms procurement on a huge scale took the place of genuine human development, with negative results that we live until today. It's worth mentioning that 60 percent of the world's arms are now bought by Arab countries.

Along with the militarisation went the wholesale persecution of communities – pre-eminently, but not exclusively, the Jewish ones in the Arab world and, of course, the Arab ones inside Israel. And this idea of homogenising societies to create, in the case of Israel, a Jewish state, in the case of the various Arab states, entirely Arab states, whether they're called Syria, Jordan, Egypt, etc., has had the most wasteful and, in my opinion, terrible results, one of the tragedies of the politics of identity which ensued. The expulsion of whole communities as a result of 1948, which set in process a system of distortion within the societies, whether it was inside Israel or in the Arab world, most of it encouraged by US policy at the time, seems to me to have led to every conceivable disaster in the way of human formations and social institutions.

Nor was this all. In the name of military security, in countries like Egypt, there was a bloody-minded, imponderably wasteful campaign against dissenters, mostly on the left, but independently minded people too, whose vocation as critics and skilled men and women was brutally terminated in prisons, fatal torture and summary executions. As one looks back at those things in the context of 1948, it's the immense panorama of waste and cruelty that stands out as the immediate result of the war itself.

Jerusalem Revisited

Edward Said returns home forty-five years after the Nakba to find his family's house in Jerusalem occupied by a right-wing Christian fundamentalist and militantly pro-Zionist group.

There were four prosperous and new Arab quarters largely built during the Mandate period (1918–1948): Upper and Lower Baqaa, Talbiya, and Qatamon. I recall that during my last weeks in the fall of 1947 I had to traverse three of the security zones instituted by the British to get to St. George's School from Talbiya; by December 1947 my parents, sisters, and I had left for Egypt. My aunt Nabiha and four of her five children stayed on but experienced grave difficulties. The area they lived in was made up of unprepared and unarmed Palestinian families; by February Talbiya had been taken over by the Hagganah. Now as we drove around, looking for my family's house, I saw no Arabs, although the handsome old stone houses still bear their Arab identity.

I remembered the house itself quite clearly: two storeys, a terraced entrance, a balcony at the front, a palm tree and a large conifer as you climbed toward the front door, a spacious (and at the time) empty square, designated as a park, that lay before the room in which I was born, facing toward the King David and the YMCA. I do not recall street names from that time (there are none, it turns out) although Cousin Yousef (now in Canada) drew me a map from memory that he sent along with a copy of the title deed. Years before, I had heard that Martin Buber lived in the house for a time after 1948, but had died elsewhere. No one seemed to know what became of the house after the middle 1960s.

Our guide for the trip was George Khodr, an elderly gentleman who had been a friend of my father's and an accountant for the family business, the Palestine Educational Company. I vividly recalled the main premises (comprising a wonderful bookshop at which Abba Eban had been a regular customer): these were built against the stretch of city wall running between the Jaffa and New gates. All gone now, as we drove past the wall, and up the Mamila Road, then a bustling commercial centre, now a gigantic construction site where a Moshe Safdie settlement was being built. Khodr's family had also lived in Talbiya in a house he took us to so as to orient himself. Despite the Mediterranean foliage one might have been in an elegant Zurich suburb, so patently did Talbiya bespeak its new European personality. As we walked around, he called the names of the villas and their original Palestinian owners – Kitaneh, Sununu, Tannous, David, Haramy, Salameh – a sad roll call of the vanished past, for Mariam a reminder of the Palestinian refugees with the very same names who fetched up in Beirut during the fifties and sixties.

It took almost two hours to find the house, and it is a tribute to my cousin's memory that only by sticking very literally to his map did we finally locate it. Earlier I was detained for half an hour by the oddly familiar contours of Mr Shamir's unmistakably Arab villa, but abandoned that line of inquiry for the greater certainty of a home on Nahum Sokolow Street, 150 yards away. For there the house was, I suddenly knew, with its still impressive bulk commanding the sandy little square, now an elegant, manicured park. My daughter later told me that, using her camera with manic excitement, I reeled off twenty-six photos of the place which, irony of ironies, bore the name plate 'International Christian Embassy' at the gate. To have found my family's house now occupied not by an Israeli Jewish family, but by a right-wing Christian fundamentalist and militantly pro-Zionist group (run by a South African Boer, no less, and with a record of unsavoury involvement with the Contras to boot), this was an abrupt blow for a child of Palestinian Christian parents. Anger and melancholy took me over, so that when an American woman came out of the house holding an armful of laundry and asked if she could help, all I could blurt out was an instinctive, 'No thanks.'

The coincidence was too much for me at that point, suddenly vitalising my family's history with this astonishing serene likeness of my young father as I really never knew him, and, as I thought back to the silent Talbiya house, with its lamentably foreclosed destiny now in 'Christian' hands, that world seemed condemned to intermittent scraps and shards of memory and melancholy. I think I knew at that instant why I should have left politics and resigned from the PNC, as I did, in late 1991, and why I felt I had to return to Palestine just then. Wasn't it that the shocking medical diagnosis I received in September of a chronically insidious blood disease convinced me for the first time of a mortality I had ignored, and which I now needed to experience with my own family, at the source, so to speak, in Palestine? And then the reminder of other earlier histories starting and ending in Jerusalem seemed for me a fitting accompaniment to the ebbing of my life on the one hand, and, on the other, a concrete reminder that just as they had started and ended, I did and would too, but so too would my children, who could now see for the first time the linked narrative of our family's generations, where that story belonged but from which it had been banished.

MAHMOUD DARWISH

To Our Land

To our land,
and it is the one near the word of god,
a ceiling of clouds
To our land,
and it is the one far from the adjectives of nouns,
the map of absence
To our land,
and it is the one tiny as a sesame seed,
a heavenly horizon ... and a hidden chasm
To our land,
and it is the one poor as a grouse's wings,
holy books ... and an identity wound
To our land,
and it is the one surrounded with torn hills,
the ambush of a new past
To our land, and it is a prize of war,
the freedom to die from longing and burning
and our land, in its bloodied night,
is a jewel that glimmers for the far upon the far
and illuminates what's outside it ...
As for us, inside,
we suffocate more!

At a Train Station that Fell Off the Map

Grass, dry air, thorns, and cactus
on the iron wire. There's the shape of a thing
in the frivolity of nonshape chewing its shadow ...
a bound void ... encircled by its opposite.
And there are two doves hovering
over the roof of an abandoned room at the station
and the station is a tattoo that has melted
in the body of place. There are also two
slim cypresses like two long needles
that embroider a lemon-yellow cloud,
and a tourist woman taking photos of two scenes:
a sun that has stretched in the sea's bed
and a wooden bench that is vacant of the traveller's sack

(The hypocrite heavenly gold is bored with its own solidity)

I stood at the station, not to wait for the train
or for emotions hidden in the aesthetics of some faraway thing,
but to know how the sea went mad and the place broke
like a ceramic jar, to know where I was born and how I lived,
and how the birds migrated to the north and south.
Is what remains of me enough
for the weightless imaginary to triumph
over the corruption of fact?
Is my gazelle still pregnant?

(We have aged. O how we've aged, and the road to the sky is long)

The train used to travel like a friendly snake from Syria
to Egypt. Its whistle concealed

the husky bleats of goats from the wolves' hunger.
As if it were a mythical time that tamed wolves to befriend us.
Its smoke used to rise over the smoke of villages,
which opened up and appeared like shrubs in nature.

(Life is intuitive. Our homes and hearts have open doors)

We were kind-hearted and naïve. We said: The land is our land
and no external affliction will befall the map's heart.
And the sky is generous to us. We hardly spoke to each other
in classical Arabic, save at prayer time and on holy nights.
Our present serenaded us: Together we live!
Our past amused us: I'll come back if you need me!
We were kind-hearted and dreamy, we didn't see
tomorrow steal the past, his prey, and leave ...

(A while ago our present used to grow wheat and squash and make
the wadi dance)

I stood at the station at sunset: Are there still two women
in one woman who is polishing her thigh with lightning?
Two mythic enemy-friends and twins
on the surface of wind, one who flirts with me, and another
who wars with me? Has spilled blood ever broken
a single sword, so I can say my first Goddess is still within me?

(I believed my old song so I can disbelieve my reality)

The train was a land ship docking ... it carried us to the realistic
cities of our imagination whenever we were in need
of innocent play with destiny. Train windows possess
the magical in the ordinary: everything runs.

Trees, ideas, waves, towers run
behind us. And the lemon scent runs. The air and the rest
of things run, and the longing
to a mysterious faraway, and the heart, run.

(Everything differed and agreed)

I stood at the station, I was as abandoned as the timekeeper's
room there. I was a dispossessed man staring
at his closet and asking himself: Was that
mind, that treasure, mine? Was this
damp lapis lazuli, humidity, and nightly dew, mine?
Was I one day the butterfly's pupil
in fragility, and in audacity, and was I her mate
in metaphor at times? Was one of those days
mine? Or does memory fall ill also and catch a fever?

(I see my trace on a stone, I think it's my moon, and chant)

Another ruin and I'll snuff my memories while standing
at the station. I don't love this grass now, this
forgotten aridity, frivolous and desolate
it writes the biography of forgetting in this mercurial place.
And I don't love chrysanthemum over the tombs of prophets.
And I don't love rescuing myself through metaphor, even if
the violin wants me as an echo of myself. I only love return
to my life, for my end to become my beginning's narrative.

(Like the clang of bells, time broke here)

I stood in the sixtieth year of my wound. I stood
at the station, not to await the train or the holler

of those who return from the south to the grain
but to memorise the olive and lemon coast
in my map's history ... is all
this absence or what remains of its crumbs mine?
Did a ghost pass me by, wave from afar and disappear?
Did I ask him: Will we slaughter a gazelle
for the stranger whenever a stranger
smiles to us and casts us a greeting?

(Like a pinecone echo fell from me)

Only my intuition guides me to myself.
Two fugitive doves lay exile's eggs on my shoulder
then soar to a pale height. A tourist woman passes by
and asks me: Can I take your picture to respect the truth?
I said: What do you mean?
She said: Can I take your picture
as an extension of nature? I said: You can ... everything
is possible, and have a great evening and leave me alone
with dying ... and with my self

(Here truth has one single lonely face and that's why I'll sing)

You are you, even if you lose. In the past
you and I are two, and in tomorrow, one. The train passed
but we weren't alert, so rise up complete and optimistic,
and wait for no one here, beside yourself. Here the train fell
off the map in the middle of the coastal path. And the fires
flamed in the heart of the map, then winter
extinguished the fires, though winter was late.
We have aged, O how we've aged before we could return
to our first names:

(I say to whoever sees me through the binoculars on the watch-tower I don't see you ... I don't see you)

I see all of my place around me. I see me in the place with all
my limbs and organs. I see palm trees edit my classical
Arabic from error. I see almond blossoms,
their habits in training my song for a sudden
joy. I see my trace and follow it. I see my shadow
and lift it from the wadi with a bereaved Canaanite
woman's comb. I see what cannot be seen of attractive
flow and whole beauty in the eternity
of the hills, and don't see my snipers.

(I become my self's guest)

There are dead who light fires around their graves.
There are living who prepare dinner for their guests.
There are enough words for metaphor to rise
above incident. Whenever the place dims a copper moon
illuminates and expands it. I am my self's guest.
A hospitality that will embarrass and delight me, until I choke
on words and words choke on obstinate tears ... and the dead,
along with the living, drink immortality's mint, without
talking much about Resurrection Day

(There's no train there, and no one will wait for the train)

Our country is the map's heart. Its punctured heart
like a coin in the metal market. The last passenger from somewhere
between Syria and Egypt didn't return to pay the fare
for some extra work the sniper did ... as the strangers expected.
The last passenger didn't return and didn't carry his death

and life certificates along for the sages of Judgment Day to discern
his place in Paradise. O we were angels and fools
when we believed the banners and the horses
and that a falcon's wing will raise us up high

(My sky is an idea, and the earth is my favourite exile)

All there is to it is that I only believe my intuition.
Evidence conducts the dialogue of the impossible. The story
of creation belongs to the philosopher's long-winded
    interpretation.
My idea about the world has a malfunction
departure has caused. My eternal wound stands trial
without an impartial judge. And the judges, exhausted
by truth, tell me: All there is to it is that
traffic accidents are common: the train fell off the map
and you burned with the ember of the past: this
wasn't an invasion ...
but I say: All there is to it is that
I only believe my intuition
(I'm still alive)

Both translated by Sinan Antoon

On This Earth

On this earth what makes life worth living:
the hesitance of April
the scent of bread at dawn
an amulet made by a woman for men
Aeschylus's works
the beginnings of love
moss on a stone
the mothers standing on the thinness of a flute
and the fear of invaders of memories.
On this earth what makes life worth living:
September's end
a lady moving beyond her fortieth year without losing
any of her grace
a sun clock in a prison
clouds imitating a flock of creatures
chants of a crowd for those meeting their end smiling
and the fear of tyrants of the songs.
On this earth what makes life worth living:
on this earth stands the mistress of the earth
mother of beginnings
mother of endings
it used to be known as Palestine
it became known as Palestine
my lady:
I deserve, because you're my lady
I deserve life.

Translated by Karim Abuawad

I Am from There

I am from there and I have memories. Like any other
Man I was born. I have a mother,
A house with several windows, friends and brothers.
I have a prison cell's cold window, a wave
Snatched by seagulls, my own view, an extra blade
Of grass, a moon at word's end, a life-supply
Of birds, and an olive tree that cannot die.
I walked and crossed the land before the crossing
Of swords made a banquet-table of a body.

I come from there, and I return the sky
To its mother when it cries for her, and cry
For a cloud on its return
To recognise me. I have learned
All words befitting of blood's court to break
The rule; I have learned all the words to take
The lexicon apart for one noun's sake,
The compound I must make:
Homeland.

Translated by A.Z. Foreman

Standing Before the Ruins of Al-Birweh

Darwish was born in the village of Al-Birweh on 13 March 1941. In 1948, it was occupied and depopulated by Israeli forces. Its inhabitants became refugees, some in Lebanon, others internally displaced and designated present-absentees. In 1949, a Kibbutz was established; a year later, a settlement was built.

Like birds, I tread lightly on the earth's skin
so as not to wake the dead
I shut the door to my emotions to become my other
I don't feel that I am a stone sighing
as it longs for a cloud
Thus I tread as if I am a tourist
and a correspondent for a foreign newspaper
Of this place I choose the wind
I choose absence to describe it
Absence sat, neutral, around me
The crow saw it
Halt, my two companions!
Let us experience this place our own way:
Here, a sky fell on a stone and bled it
so that anemones would bloom in the spring
(Where is my song now?)
Here, the gazelle broke the glass of my window
so that I would follow it
(So where is my song now?)
Here, the magical morning butterflies carried the path to my school
(So where is my song now?)
Here I saddled a horse to fly to my stars
(So where is my song now?)

I say to my two companions:
Stop so that I may weigh the place
and its emptiness with *Jahili* odes
full of horses and departure
For every rhyme we will pitch a tent
For every home to be stormed by the wind,
there is a rhyme
But I am the son of my first tale
My milk is warm in my mother's breast
The bed is swung by two tiny birds
My father is building my tomorrow with his two hands
I didn't grow up and so did not go to exile
The tourist says: Wait for the dove to finish its cooing!
I say: It knows me and I know it, but the letter has not arrived
The journalist interrupts my secret song:
Do you see that dairy factory behind that strong pine tree?
I say: No, I only see the gazelle at the window
He says: What about the modern roads on the rubble of houses?
I say: No, I don't see them
I only see the garden under them
and I see the cobweb
He says: Dry your two tears with a handful of fresh grass
I say: That is my other crying over my past
The tourist says: The visit is over
I haven't found anything to photograph except a ghost
I say: I see absence with all its instruments
I touch it and hear it. It lifts me high
I see the ends of the distant skies
Whenever I die I notice
I am born again and I return
from absence to absence.

Translated by Sinan Antoon

SAMIH AL-QASSIM

So What If

O my country, an earring left to swing
From the ear of the earth with no rest;
My country ... a woman whose thighs are spread
Wide by a wind from the West,
My country the raft's one oar,
My country the missing son!
Will you one day rise up in my breast?
Will you become a country ... like the rest?

The End of a Discussion with a Prison Guard

Through the eyehole of this little cell of mine
I can see the trees all smiling at me,
The rooftops crowded with my family,
The windows breaking into tears for me
And prayers for me.
Through the eyehole of this little cell of mine
I see your bigger cell just fine.

Kafr Qassim

On 29 October 1956, the Israeli authorities declared a 5PM curfew in Palestinian villages, bolstered with a shoot-to-kill order. Villagers working in the fields failed to receive word of this. Forty-eight Palestinians were killed when they tried to return.

No monument raised, no memorial, and no rose.
Not one line of verse to ease the slain
Not one curtain, not one blood-stained
Shred of our blameless brothers' clothes.
Not one stone to engrave their names.
Not one thing. Only the shame.

Their circling ghosts have still not ceased
Digging up graves in Kafr Qasim's debris.

Travel Tickets

The day I'm killed,
my killer, rifling through my pockets,
will find travel tickets:
One to peace,
one to the fields and the rain,
and one
to the conscience of humankind.

Dear killer of mine, I beg you:
Do not stay and waste them.
Take them, use them.
I beg you to travel.

All translated by A.Z. Foreman

Persona Non Grata

Here is the beginning of carnage.
Its finale: my lunar scream.
I understand my glass can be fragmented by a bullet. Aim well and try to assassinate *me*. My little ones are too young for death, crude fruit unbecoming for your masters. Aim well: my wife is safe now in her kitchen. Aim well, here I am alone reading *Le Fou d'Elsa*. If your sniper bends two inches he can see me: a quiet figure beside the study window.
Do come.
Do come with all the dreadful fires of your malice.

Do come! Here I have a spiral ladder linking heaven to earth, a fan failing in the heat, a tank strolling on a pregnant belly, and here I have barren nations.
Skulls mounted with medals in the stock exchange of death, shoes inhabited by scorpions. Oh, for a glass of sour bitter water in exchange for my blood and tears. I have been wounded: my wound is vivid, my voice is vivid, my silence is vivid. I bow my heart in respect. Do come.
My affliction: dazzlement.
My wrath: supplication.
Do come.
Do come.
My stay is flight.
My death is combat.
I swear by fig and oil, by silence and clamour, by fertility and sterility, by honey and hemlock, by bud and blood, by ignorance and knowledge, yesterday and today, I swear to fight.
I will continue to fight!
I will continue!
Until truth is born and falsehood is vanished
I will and will, rise and sink, round and surround, release and refrain, hover and halt.
What? How?
Thus it is:
a fall on to the peak of death,
stallions trotting behind in the tracks of tragicomedy.
Thus it is:
resting into a siesta on a bus seat – an enclosed prison cell.
Menstruation with sterility, sterility with menstruation, sorrow and protest, love and hate: a wasteland resort.
I will walk out of my body ... I cannot bear it!
I will search for a friend.

I will depart from my step ... I cannot bear it!
I will search for a road.
There is no road but me
and these are my steps.
In my body is the next step.
[...]
Whither go the doves?
Whence come the waves of swallows?
Forbidden to me to cross again and again the threshold of my questions, forbidden to me my food and drink.
If I do not restore the markings of my face and recover the flame of pride
Forbidden to me my land.
Forbidden to me my sky.
Fashionable freaks flutter around my grave, having dropped time.
They said: Do you sing?
I said: I will sing in the name of him who kills the awaited life.
In the name of my beginning and end
And a song strangled with string.
I will sing my second elegy,
the geography of distant words and elevated images.
I will sing my flesh on bloody roads
and the Book of my exodus from the cruel paradise.
I will sing to my name,
I will sing in my name,
and in my name the sea swallows the crew of a lost submarine.
And the death storm sings its splendid melodies.
In my name, my name is written on water
and my body is erased on water.
They said and I said.
They assailed and I assaulted.
I am the problem.

The sniper of Beirut tarried. Death spared me in my exile, my homeland, my shroud, my Golgotha.
There is no solution, warring or peaceful ... I am the problem.

I am: the songs and the wheat buds, the cannons and the bombs.
There is no good without me
and no evil without me.

I am: the impossible possible the beautiful ugly the tall short the intruding enemy the honorable friend the lowly mighty the noble rogue the serious boor the slim stout the sand palm the lightning flood the desert ruin
I am the sky scrapers the sky the absence the advent the ascent the descent
I am the impossible possible
There is no shade but me
No form but me
no solution but me
My burden is as large as my back
My back is as large as my life
My life is as large as my patience
And my patience is graceful, graceful
And my patience is spacious, spacious.

Translated by Ferial Ghazoul

FADWA TUQAN

Hamza

Hamza was just an ordinary man
like others in my hometown
who work only with their hands for bread.

When I met him the other day,
this land was wearing a cloak of mourning
in windless silence. And I felt defeated.
But Hamza-the-ordinary said:
'My sister, our land has a throbbing heart,
it doesn't cease to beat, and it endures
the unendurable. It keeps the secrets
of hills and wombs. This land sprouting
with spikes and palms is also the land
that gives birth to a freedom-fighter.
This land, my sister, is a woman.'

Days rolled by. I saw Hamza nowhere.
Yet I felt the belly of the land
was heaving in pain.

Hamza – sixty-five – weighs
heavy like a rock on his own back.
'Burn, burn his house,'
a command screamed,

'and tie his son in a cell.'
The military ruler of our town later explained:
it was necessary for law and order,
that is, for love and peace!

Armed soldiers besieged his house:
the serpent's coil came full circle.
The bang at the door was but an order –
'evacuate, damn it!'
And generous as they were with time, they could say:
'in an hour, yes!'

Hamza opened the window.
Face to face with the sun blazing outside,
he cried: 'in this house my children
and I will live and die
for Palestine.'
Hamza's voice echoed clean
across the bleeding silence of the town.

An hour later, impeccably,
the house came crumbling down,
the rooms were blown to pieces in the sky,
and the bricks and the stones all burst forth,
burying dreams and memories of a lifetime
of labour, tears, and some happy moments.

Yesterday I saw Hamza
walking down a street in our town –
Hamza the ordinary man as he always was:
always secure in his determination.

Labour Pains

The wind blows the pollen in the night
through ruins of fields and homes.
Earth shivers with love,
with the pain of giving birth,
but the conqueror wants us to believe
stories of submission and surrender.

O Arab Aurora!
Tell the usurper of our land
that childbirth is a force unknown to him,
the pain of a mother's body,
that the scarred land
inaugurates life
at the moment of dawn
when the rose of blood
blooms on the wound.

The Deluge and The Tree

When the hurricane swirled and spread its deluge
of dark evil
onto the good green land
'they' gloated. The western skies
reverberated with joyous accounts:
'The Tree has fallen!
The great trunk is smashed! The hurricane leaves no life in the Tree!'

Had the Tree really fallen?
Never! Not with our red streams flowing forever,
not while the wine of our thorn limbs
fed the thirsty roots,
Arab roots alive
tunnelling deep, deep, into the land!

When the Tree rises up, the branches
shall flourish green and fresh in the sun,
the laughter of the Tree shall leaf
beneath the sun
and birds shall return.
Undoubtedly, the birds shall return.
The birds shall return.

Excerpt from Call of the Land

I ask nothing more
Than to die in my country
To dissolve and merge with the grass,
To give life to a flower
That a child of my country will pick,
All I ask
Is to remain in the bosom of my country
As soil,
Grass,
A flower.

All translated by Tania Tamari Nasir and Christopher Millis

TAWFIQ ZAYYAD

I Call to You

I call to you
I clasp your hands
And kiss the earth beneath your feet
And I say to you: I sacrifice myself for you
And dedicate the light of my eyes to you
And the warmth of the heart, I give you ...
The tragedy is that I live
My share of tragedy is that of yours
I call to you
I clasp your hands
I have not spared myself for my homeland or underestimated the
power of my hands
I have stood in the face of my oppressors
Orphaned, naked and barefooted ...
I have carried my blood on my palm
And have not lowered my flag
And I have protected the green grass above the tombs of my
ancestors
I call to you, I call to you ...

Translated by Atef Alshaer

We Shall Remain

As if twenty impossibles we are
In Al-Lid, Ar-Ramleh and the Galilee
Here ... on your chests, staying as a wall
Remaining we are
In your throats
Like a piece of glass, like cactus
And in your eyes
A storm of fire
Here ... on your chests, staying as a wall
Remaining we are
Hungry we get ... naked ... we challenge ...
Chant poems
Fill the street with angry demonstrations
Fill prisons with pride
Produce children ... a revolting generation ...
after generation
As if twenty impossibles we are
In Al-Lid, Ar-Ramleh and the Galilee

* * *

Plant ideas, like yeast in dough
The coldness of the Galilee in our nerves
Live coal ... hell in our hearts
If thirsty we get rocks we squeeze
If hungry we get soil we eat ... and we never leave
Our redolent blood we don't spare ...
We don't spare ... we don't spare ...
Here we have a past ...
A present ...
And a future

Translated by Adib S. Kawar

On The Trunk of an Olive Tree

Because I do not weave wool,
And daily am in danger of detention,
And my house is the object of police visits
To search and 'to cleanse',
Because I cannot buy paper,
I shall carve the record of my sufferings,
And all my secrets
On an olive tree
In the courtyard
Of my house.
I shall carve my story and the chapters of my tragedy,
I shall carve my sighs
On my grove and on the tombs of my dead;
I shall carve
All the bitterness I have tasted,
To be blotted out by some of the happiness to come
I shall carve the number of each deed
Of our usurped land
The location of my village and its boundaries.
The demolished houses of its peoples,
My uprooted trees,
And each crushed wild blossom.
And the names of those master torturers
Who rattled my nerves and caused my misery.
The names of all the prisons,
And every type of handcuff
That closed around my wrists,
The files of my jailers,
Every curse
Poured upon my head.

I shall carve:
Kafr Qasim, I shall not forget!
And I shall carve:
Deir Yassin, it's rooted in my memory.
I shall carve:
We have reached the peak of our tragedy.
It has absorbed us and we have absorbed it,
But we have finally reached it.
I shall carve all that the sun tells me,
And what the moon whispers,
And what the skylark relates,
Near the well
Forsaken by lovers.

And to remember it all,
I shall continue to carve
All the chapters of my tragedy,
And all the stages of the disaster,
From beginning
To end,
On the olive tree
In the courtyard
Of the house.

Translated by Abdel Wahhab el-Messiri

MUIN BSEISO

'NO!'

His wounds said: 'No!'
His chains said: 'No!'
And the turtledove which shielded his wound with her feather
Said: 'No!'
'No!' for those who sold and bought
Gaza's silver anklet.
They sold the bullets and bought a goose.
Quaking goose!
Stop for a moment.
And listen to him
Saying: 'No!'
Pity him; he did not die under neon lights,
Between the candlestick and the moon.
Pity him; there was no formal announcement
or a dumb funeral.
No moaning poem nor song.
Stones!
Let me compose, if only one line of verse,
That I may recite it to all the men with long and false beards.
Stop quaking for a moment
And listen to him saying: 'No!'
Like the solid fence of a house in Gaza.
Every day, he gets killed one thousand times,
Quaking goose!

Translated by Abdul Wahab Al-Messiri

The Vinegar Cup

Cast your lots, people,
Who'll get my robe
After crucifixion?

The vinegar cup in my right hand,
The thorn crown on my head,
And the murderer has walked away free
While your son has been led
To the cross.
But I shall not run
From the vinegar cup,
Nor the crown of thorns
I'll carve the nails of my cross from my own bones
And continue,
Spilling drops of my blood onto this earth
For if I should not rip apart
How would you be born from my heart?
How would I be born from your heart?
Oh, my people!

Translated by May Jayyusi and Naomi Shihab Nye

RASHID HUSSEIN

Without a Passport

I was born without a passport
I grew up
and saw my country
become prisons
without a passport
So I raised a country
a sun
and wheat
in every house
I tended to the trees therein
I learned how to write poetry
to make the people of my village happy
without a passport
I learned that he whose land is stolen
does not like the rain
If he were ever to return to it, he will
without a passport
But I am tired of minds
that have become hotels
for wishes that never give birth
except with a passport
Without a passport
I came to you
and revolted against you

so slaughter me
perhaps I will then feel that I am dying
without a passport

Translated by Sinan Antoon

Against

Against my country's rebels wounding a sapling
Against a child – any child – bearing a bomb
Against my sister studying a rifle's components
Against what you will –
But even a prophet becomes powerless
When his vision takes in
the murderers' horses
Against a child becoming a hero at ten
Against a tree's heart sprouting mines
Against my orchard's branches becoming gallows
Against erecting scaffolds among the roses of my land
Against what you will –
But after my country, my comrades, and my youth were burnt,
How can my poems not turn into guns?

Translated by May Jayyusi and Naomi Shihab Nye

TAHA MUHAMMAD ALI

Exodus

The street is empty
as a monk's memory,
and faces explode in the flames
like acorns –
and the dead crowd the horizon
and doorways.
No vein can bleed
more than it already has,
no scream will rise
higher than it's already risen.
We will not leave!

Everyone outside is waiting
for the trucks and the cars
loaded with honey and hostages.
We will not leave!
The shields of light are breaking apart
before the rout and the siege;
outside, everyone wants us to leave.
But we will not leave!

Ivory white brides
behind their veils
slowly walk in captivity's glare, waiting,

and everyone outside wants us to leave,
but we will not leave!

The big guns pound the jujube groves,
destroying the dreams of the violets,
extinguishing bread, killing the salt,
unleashing thirst
and parching lips and souls.
And everyone outside is saying:
'What are we waiting for?
Warmth we're denied,
the air itself has been seized!
Why aren't we leaving?'
Masks fill the pulpits and brothels,
the places of ablution.
Masks cross-eyed with utter amazement;
they do not believe what is now so clear,
and fall, astonished,
writhing like worms, or tongues.
We will not leave!

Are we in the inside only to leave?
Leaving is just for the masks,
for pulpits and conventions.
Leaving is just
for the siege-that-comes-from-within,
the siege that comes from the Bedouin's loins,
the siege of the brethren
tarnished by the taste of the blade
and the stink of crows.
We will not leave!

Outside they're blocking the exits
and offering their blessings to the impostor,
praying, petitioning
Almighty God for our deaths.

Translated by Peter Cole, Yahya Hijazi and Gabriel Levin

SALEM JUBRAN

Refugee

The sun crosses borders
without any solider shooting at it
The nightingale sings in Tulkarm
of an evening
eats and roosts peacefully
with kibbutzim birds.
A stray donkey grazes
across the firing line
in peace
and on one aim.
But I, your son made refugee
Oh my native land –
between me and your horizons
the frontier walls stand.

Translated by Lena Jayyusi and Naomi Shihab Nye

AHMAD DAHBOUR

The Prison

To Abu Faris ... who has been there

Prison teaches that the heart is a desert,
That light is a desert.
It curses the fire and the land of the commandos.
Prison teaches that water is a chameleon,
That the landscape is a snake,
That echo is treacherous, and the wind an enemy.
Prison teaches that the guide's sight grows dim,
And that the homeland departs.
Prison is a black kingdom in the sand;
Prison is a sword guarding the eyelids;
Prison ... not the homeland!
So how, my beloved homeland, will the beloved ones survive?
Here we are, no complaints and no regrets,
We never say: an aimless wandering!
Blood gushes forth from the depths of our love.
Prison assaults but does not hit the mark;
Our wounds hit back,
Reaching out like water ... like the wilderness,
Promising the light with a new light.
From deep within us, signalling twice!
Our cub child,
And the fire of salvation.
We see it, yes we do.

We are not dreaming,
We almost step into his joyous landscape
We almost do.
This is the moment of travail in our difficult labour,
We hug the new-born –
He who springs from our very ecstasy,
Whose kicks we feel in our guts,
Who teaches the hungry what he knows
And declares in words well understood:
Revolution, revolution ... till life.
The inmate has not lost his features in the sand,
Prison did not turn him into a desert.
From his hunger, water and vegetation sprang.
When silence wounds him,
He can break it with a sigh,
But he endures.
His testimony:
Near death, there were exhaustion and fatigue,
His executioner pressing him to promise
A word ... a groan, or to divulge his secret,
But all in vain.
His countenance was radiating in the sand
Like an oasis,
For prison had not turned him into a desert.

New Suggestions

Out of what lair did the earthly tyrants escape?
Nero burned Rome twice, then composed a discordant tune
he went on playing till the city sang with him.
Hulaku who inherited that melody
set fire
to the world's library, the river ran
with ink, and from the ashes was born
the language of the locusts which rose
to thank the madman.
After the salutations to madness, Hitler came
(...) but unable to be appeased,
had to include the sea
in his vital destruction,
and war at sea, turmoil on land,
combined in their angry conflagration.
I too have seen a tyrant –
whose power diminished the other three.
he has committed every atrocity,
and yet: in his day,
there were five poets,
who took to silence.

Both translated by A.M. Elmessiri

MAY SAYIGH

Departure

In this moment of departure,
point your red arrows,
disarm the lightning, and open wide
the gate to my exile.
Close the sky's open face, and ride away.
I long so deeply that the shores unfold their seas
and horses bolt!
Now I'll carry the roads and palm trees in my suitcase,
I'll lock my tears in the evening's copybooks
and seal the seasons.

Let's begin our song: here is Beirut wearing you
like her own clothes.
You must sit well on the surface of her glory
abandoning tears
In her blue froth
She contains you like eternity
like the sense of beginning that comes with certainty.

How can you be dead, yet so absolutely present?

Let the rivers abandon their skies,
and the seas dry out!
Everything in the universe has an end

except my spilt blood ...

Each time I think of it
You remain as large as your death.
The war planes choose you, discover you, plant
their blackness in you.
From all those clouded last visions,
how will you begin the story of harvest?
We planes select you,
at the start of your sleep,
at the end of your sleep.
How often did the sky explode over you
with hatred?
How often were you taken aside?
How many massacres did you survive?
Now you collect all the wounds, taking refuge with
death,
wearing dreams as wings.

Translated by Lena Jayyusi and Naomi Shihab Nye

IZZUDDIN MANASRA

Dawn Visitors

At the entries to capital cities I met him,
distracted and sad,
a man with worry lines
that weighed him down
like a cypress tree, drooping and silent,
despite the winds that ruffled him
whispering in the evenings –
but he would not answer the wind.
At the gates of capital cities – I cannot name them
but I sing their Arabic names when troubles reign –
I call on the capitals when shells are slaughtering my people's
children. I call on them, I scream, but no one
answers.
They've all travelled west, and north. I wish
They'd gone east, I wish
They'd become stars in exile, servants to strangers.
At harvest time they sang under the pine trees
but none of the harvests was theirs.
it is for those hard-hearted men
who owns the land of exile
Don't bury me in any Arab capital, they've all tortured me
for so long,
giving me nothing but death and suffering and poverty
and the martyred neighbours of my grave,

those new kinsmen, for every stranger is kinsman to the stranger.
No, don't bury me in any Arab capital
at the mercy of this ordeal!

At the gate of the capitals I met him
his head forever bent,
immortal as the earth of Hebron,
proud as the mountains of Safad.
He was soft like old wine when it steeps inside the body.

I would have tempted the stars
to accompany his beautiful departure,
a star to guard him, and one lovely maiden
to tend him forever.

Translated by Atef Alshaer

SAHAR KHALIFEH

Excerpt from Wild Thorns

Um Sabir was shouting, 'Hey, Itaf! Ask Um Badawi if she's got any spare flour.'

As the child made her way across the roof, an Israeli solider shouted, 'Get down! Get Down! You can't go up there.'

Um Sabir beat her breast in distress. 'What a wretched life! How can I feed my children? It's enough to break your heart, this life! What'll we do if the curfew goes on for another two days?'

All over the old part of town, the women gathered at their windows trying to borrow whatever they could from each other. The situation was desperate. Most of those who lived in the old neighbourhood were labourers, greengrocers, butchers, or sellers of falafel and tam'iyya; they were generally poor and kept nothing in store. The children were cooped up inside the small houses, driving their mothers mad. One child was under a bed, another on top of a cupboard, a baby was screaming, husbands were venting their anger on their innocent wives.

Abu Sabir murmured, 'Forgive us, Oh Lord, deliver us!' Zuhdi cursed the day he'd been spared the sandstorms of Kuwait. 'I'll go crazy if I ever taste lentils again,' he said, and threw his slipper at one of the children; this brought a chorus of wails from all sides. 'God curse whoever fathered you, you curs!' he shouted. His wife Saadiyya suddenly opened the door, letting the children run free. 'Out!' she yelled. 'Get out! Go and pester the Jews instead of getting on my nerves!' Um Sabir did the same and her husband exploded: ' You're crazy, woman! The streets are full of Jewish soldiers!'

But children were now emerging from all the houses, at first lurking in dark corners like mice, staring out at the soldiers and laughing and winking at one another. The soldiers wore helmets and carried machine-guns. A little boy ran from one house to the next, and a soldier yelled and swore at him. The children's laughter echoed down the street as they imitated the soldier's oaths. Another boy tied a tomato can to a cat's tail and sent the animal running. A soldier swung and pointed his gun at the boy. But the children, delighted at the game, laughed even louder. The soldiers began to chase the boys, who scampered home, slamming the doors behind them. Then out they came slamming the doors behind them. Then out they came again. A soldier caught one of them and started to beat him, and the mothers let loose a stream of curses on all who'd had a hand in the creation of the state. Their husbands blinked in surprise at the volleys of oaths.

A tank passed, all four sides bristling with guns; the weight of its metal tracks crushed the old paving stones. The children shrank deeper into the shadowy corners of the houses till the tank had gone, then ran out after it, chanting: 'Fatah! ... PLO ... Fatah! ... PLO ...' The soldiers shouted curses and aimed their weapons at the children, sending them dashing for cover again. But a little boy of six stood his ground, unzipped his faded trousers and pointed his penis at the soldiers, as though affirming the principle of self-defence. The streets exploded in an uproar of shouts as the boys seemed suddenly filled with insane bravado. A soldier seized two of them by the scruffs of the neck and dangled them like a pair of plucked pigeons. After thrashing them soundly, he pushed them both into a patrol car. The girls began to beat out a rhythm on empty margarine cans. And the boys went on screaming out the PLO slogan: 'Revolution! Revolution until victory! Revolution!

Revolution until victory!'

Um Sabir leaned half-way out of the window and yelled at the soldier who was mistreating the children: 'May God break your arm! May seventy evil eyes get you! May your children die young! May God destroy you, by the glory of the Prophet Muhammad!'

The children chanting and clapping rang through the empty streets, a crescendo of rhyming slogans about God, Palestine, Arab unity, the Popular Front, The Democratic Front, freedom, dedication, self-sacrifice and Yasser Arafat.

But throughout the din, engineers of the so-called Israeli Defence Forces went on measuring the height and width of an old house at the end of the street. People ran out of the doomed house, the men with beds and mattresses from their neighbours' houses. And then everything went quiet. People hid in the corners of their homes, their windows open but their ears tightly shut. Then came the explosion.

The walls of the old house crumbled. In one massive piece, the roof caved in and settled on the rubble. The old man whose house it had been stood on a neighbouring roof and called out the Adhan, his voice breaking: 'Allahu Akbar, God is most great!'

'God is most great!' repeated the neighbours in unison. Gathered at the windows, the women raised their voices in loud ululations, while the girls continued to beat out a rhythm on the empty tin cans. A single piercing girlish voice began the song of solidarity once again. The boys took up the melody until the whole street was filled with the cry, 'Palestine! Palestine!'

Usama, watching from a window, found he had tears in his eyes. So all was well, in fact. He saw Basil standing in a corner alternately chanting: 'We're all men of Yasser Arafat' and 'Revolution! Revolution until victory!'

Two soldiers grabbed Basil, who offered little resistance. They covered his head a sackcloth of hood and shoved him into a petrol car, while his sister Nuwar stared dumbfounded from a window. 'Whatever God wills, so be it,' his father could be heard shouting. 'But what came over the boy? Does he think he can free Palestine all by himself?' The boy's mother burst into tears. Nuwar looked coldly at her father's frozen face, then turned back to the window as though to reassure herself that the children had not been cowed, but were still energetically beating their drums and chanting:

'Kalashnikovs will destroy the tanks!
RPGs will bring down the warplanes!'

Translated by Trevor LeGassick and Elizabeth Fernea

SALMA KHADRA JAYYUSI

Excerpt from Without Roots

I

The ringing burst loud and frightening
Then that voice persistent and sad:
'Send your aid eastwards
All your uncles have become refugees.'
I heaved a deep sigh and grieved sorely over them
Then I sent my uncles clothes
Which I had piled up for beggars
Raisins which I had but we would not eat
Sticky piasters with no bright sheen or ringing jingle
And tears and tears and tears and a groan.

Since that day I gave my piasters to no beggar
For my cousins had become refugees.

II

My uncle hungered and lamented his hunger
Then we fed him for a month as a guest
And rested from the pangs of conscience
We then gave him up to the great wide world
And got absorbed in our own worlds.
'Many a dove calling in the forenoon's stirred our sadness

And we remembered him and plunged in tears
And rest from the pangs of conscience.
Who frightened away the white-legged horses from their hills?
Who toppled down their riders? Who feeds them in their nakedness?
Who knows the green summits?
A strong noble people was living there then ... went astray ...

III

Pale lips do not approach prayer at dawn
Pale lips do not know the purity of kisses
They do not kiss today except their lust
And though their feverish passion bears fruit
Pale lips do not kiss naked children
Born without roots, without a marrow,
From a passion that has no love.

O sons of the dead, are you dead like them
Or are you orphans? Or the scar of a wound in a sad people?
We are all that ...
A word of a hoarse discordant tone united us
'refugees'

Translated by Issa J. Boullata

SALMAN ABU SITTA

Mapping My Return

News started to trickle down from the north, particularly Jaffa and Tel Aviv. Those who had work or relatives in the north started to return home. They said that Jews were attacking more and more villages, blowing up buses, burning houses, and expelling people.

Who were these people? They were not our neighbours and certainly not our friends. People said they were a motley assortment of Jews imported from across the sea. They called them 'vagabonds of the world'. What did they look like? Those who had seen them close up said they wore a variety of odd uniforms, quite unlike those in the British army. They did not all look the same: some were blond, some swarthy, some dark, and some looked Inglizi. They spoke a babble of languages – English, French, Russian, Hungarian, Romanian, and Spanish, to name but a few. Sometimes they used what was thought of as a secret language, like a code or cipher; it was *ibrani*, or Hebrew. Those who came from the north said these people were not Awlad Arab, or Arab Jews, who spoke Arabic like us. They were ruthless, unruly and vicious, and they hated the Arabs. They did not know the country, but they always carried with them detailed maps, no doubt obtained from the British.

***

Finally the Jewish attacks reached us in the south.

The Jews wanted to test our defences. They attacked our land in al-Ma'in on 8, 10 and 12 May 1948. About a dozen fighters with rifles, one machine gun, and one Boys anti-tank rifle, held them off; meanwhile the Zionists burned piles of harvested wheat and killed cattle. Their main target was to cut off the railway line at Deir al-Balah Station, which was located near the Kfar Darom colony. The planned date was 15 May 1948: the end of the British Mandate and day that the Egyptian forces were expected to enter Palestine. And of course we did not know it at the time, but the day before, on the afternoon of 14 May, had come the unilateral declaration of Israel's statehood.

Meanwhile, the planned attack on the railway would not only cause major disruption to the Egyptian forces, but it would have been a huge embarrassment to King Farouk who was about to visit his forces. To cut off the railway, the Jews had to conquer al-Ma'in first. They were well prepared and knew that al-Ma'in was a Palestinian stronghold. In the late hours of 14 May, Hamed, [my cousin returning from university to fight] in his observation post, saw row upon row of headlights advancing toward us. Surprised, he fired one shot from his flare gun to warn us. A green light rose on the horizon: the wrong signal. He corrected himself by sending two red ones into the air. Hamed's contraptions delayed the Jewish troops for some hours, but in the end they detonated his mines and crossed over his ditches on planks.

On the ridge, facing us four kilometres away, lay the shrine of Sheikh Nuran, a venerated *weli*, a revered saint. Wadi Shallalah, where Hamed was stationed, was beyond Sheikh Nuran's shrine on low-lying land. When Jewish troops had passed the temporary obstacle of Hamed's mines and trenches, they ascended the Nuran ridge and came into full view.

'Oh my sons, the Jews are coming to take you. The Jews are coming,' cried Abdullah's mother. An old woman and a light sleeper, she was overwhelmed by the sight of a long line of lights probing the darkness. There, on the near horizon, we saw the headlights of twenty-four armoured vehicles approaching us. A monster with forty-eight eyes faced us, with the ominous roar of its engines.

About fifteen young men, including Hamed, assembled quickly and fired their rifles toward the advancing column, without much effect. The main force of about a dozen men was stationed at the school, forming the second line of defence. The men at the school were armed with rifles, but Mousa [my brother] had a Browning machine-gun and Ibrahim [my brother] a Boys, which could penetrate an armoured car. These were the most powerful armaments we had.

The defence party was on high ground facing the Nuran ridge. Their hail of bullets, especially the threat of the Boys, stopped the advancing Jewish armoured vehicles in their tracks for a while as they assessed the situation. Then the Zionists split into two groups: twelve armoured vehicles veered toward Nuran ridge and the remaining twelve advanced directly toward the defence party on my father's land, where the school, the house, and the farm stood.

At the school building, Salman Abu Suleiman, my father's cousin, recklessly stood on the roof and started shooting his old rifle. Mousa, with hardly any experience, kept his finger on the trigger of the machine-gun until it overheated and jammed. Ibrahim, on the Boys, must have hit at least one tank, or so the confusion of the headlights indicated.

The tanks had overrun Hamed and his small group, but they, our first line of defence, kept shooting at them from behind, moving from one side to another.

Women and children ran in a northerly direction. Mothers tried to locate their children in the darkness. They tried hurriedly to pick up things their children needed: milk, blankets, and the like. In the background, the threatening lights, the hail of bullets tracing arcs in the sky, the hurried confusion, the agonising cries, and the shouts for a missing child heightened our fear of impending death.

My mother led my sister and me in the darkness. 'Where are you?'

'I am here,' I cried back.

'Where? Where?' she pleaded.

All the women and children knew where to go. They all headed towards Wadi Farha, a deep ravine and a dry riverbed in the summer. In the winter, its bed carried rainwater that filled the wells. I knew this wadi well; it had steep sides that were several times my height. It was a place where I often hid and went on wild adventures, with galloping horses, monsters, and demons. But that night – or dawn – was different. It was not a flight of childish fantasy. The thud of Zionist bombs, the crying children, and the frightened mothers were the elements of a real nightmare. Women splashed dirt on their faces to discourage rape.

Our schoolteacher, Muhammad Abu Liyya, was an affable young man, liked by everyone. A man of learning, he did not carry a gun. He fled to the wadi. Finding himself among women and children, he felt ashamed and ran for safety toward the village of Beni Suheila, leaving his wife behind.

On the way, he ran into the grand old man, Hajj Mahmoud, Hamed's father, on his horse, returning from Beni Suheila.

'Ya Hajj, al-yahud! The Jews!'

Hajj Mahmoud was hard of hearing. 'Huh?'

'Yahud! Yahud!'

'Huh?'

Abu Liyya sped on his way, repeating the same warning. Hamed's father continued on his way toward the battle site, unaware of the danger ahead. When he came closer, he realised what was happening. Hamed had not yet emerged from the battle and was assumed dead. Later the next day, he saw Hamed in terrible shape, but alive. The grand old man wept. 'I had never seen him cry before,' Hamed remarked later.

During the night in the wadi, we were worried about what had become of the men, our fathers and brothers. With the first light, we could recognise objects. Someone peered out of the ravine:

'Look at the smoke!'

'Oh, that's the school. It's gone!' A column of smoke was billowing from the direction of the school that my father had built in 1920. I felt a bomb explode in my guts. There was another explosion and a column of smoke rose up. 'That's the *bayyara* (orchard)', someone shouted.

Our house, all the homes, had gone up in smoke. Columns of smoke, announcing the destruction of our landscape, were rising into the sky. Their peculiar shape and distant smell filled us with grief. Still, the concern was for the people. Women started wailing and beating their cheeks in anticipation of bad news.

By midday, the shooting had stopped. Twelve tanks continued westward toward Deir al-Balah. We remained hiding in the wadi. Half of the Jewish tanks were still there. A light airplane was hovering overhead most of the day. It seemed that the destruction of the Zionist convoy at Deir al-Balah had been reported. The remaining convoy that had stayed in al-Ma'in retreated to its base, leaving only the smouldering remains of their work.

Slowly we emerged from our hiding place and began inspecting the charred ruins. My brothers Ibrahim and Mousa emerged, to our joy, alive and well. They told us about how they had been surrounded. They had retreated to the *karm*, my father's orchard, with its cactus fence. The enemy thought they had them cornered inside the fence, but the defenders escaped from the other side of the *karm* through hidden gaps in the cactus fence. Still, we had lost a number of fighters, and found many in a ditch, dead. My father was not in al-Ma'in; he had gone to Khan Yunis. Abdullah [the resistance leader] had gone two days earlier to the Egyptian border to meet General Mawawi, the commanding officer of the Egyptian forces, coming to save us.

We found corpses here and there. The two shops owned by al-Shawwal and Abu I'teim stood wide open, their shelves empty. Near the *bayyara* we found Muhammad Abu Juma lying dead, spattered with blood. Poor man, he was a simple, peaceful young person, who never carried a gun or even knew how to use one.

We spent the following night and day taking in the shock and contemplating what to do. My father and Abdullah, whose direction and counsel we were waiting for, returned. Abdullah said the Egyptian forces had now entered Palestine and 'our rescue was imminent'. He told us that when he offered to join the army with his group, General Mawawi replied, 'Leave the business of war to the professionals.'

'We can show you the way. We can be the front line. We can keep an eye on and surround the colonies,' Abdullah insisted. He received no response from the Egyptian general.

My father told my brother Mousa to return to his university and urged Hamed to do the same, leaving the fighting to 'the professionals'. I stood there looking helpless. My Beersheba school was out of bounds, my old school destroyed. My father came up with the solution: 'Take your brother with you,' he instructed Mousa.

We bade a tearful farewell to mother and father and the few family members who were still there. It was a subdued good-bye, without the anticipation of expected adventure that would normally accompany a journey like this, or the assurance that those whom we left behind would be there when we returned.

Hamed, Mousa and I rode to the Khan Yunis railway station. I rode behind Mousa. We carried nothing with us, no clothes, no papers, just the few pounds my father had slipped into Mousa's hand. I looked back at the smouldering ruins, at the meadows of my childhood, golden with the still-unharvested wheat.

I was engulfed by a feeling of both anxiety and serenity: serenity because we were still alive and an anxiety that was never to leave me. I wanted to know who this faceless enemy was. What did they look like, why did they hate us, why did they destroy us, why had they had literally burned our lives to the ground? What had we done to them? Who were these Jews anyway? I thought to myself that I must find out who they were: their names, their faces, where they came from. I must know their army formations, their officers, what exactly they had done that day, and where they lived later.

I scanned the horizon behind me, recalling the places where I was born, played, went to school, as they slowly disappeared from view. My unexpected departure did not feel that it would be such a long separation – it was simply a sojourn in another place for a while. If the future was vague for me at that moment, the past that I had just left behind became frozen in my mind and became my present forever.

I never imagined that I would not see these places again, that I would never be able to return to my birthplace. The events of those two days catapulted us into the unknown. I spent the rest of my life on a long, winding journey of return, a journey that has taken me to dozens of countries over decades of travel and turned my black hair to silver. But like a boomerang, I knew the end destination, and that the only way to it was the road of return I had decided to take ...

GHADA KARMI

Excerpt from In Search of Fatima

My father got back into the car and my mother said, "Why can't they make up their minds? One minute they tell us all the women and children are to leave and now they're saying we shouldn't. And anyway, what's the point now with everyone already gone?' My father told her to keep her voice down. As we started to move off, I twisted round on Fatima's knee and looked out of the back window. And there to my horror was Rex standing in the middle of the road. We can't have closed the gate properly and he must somehow have managed to get out. He stood still, his head up, his tail stiff, staring after our receding car.

'Look!' I cried out frantically, 'Rex has got out. Stop, please, he'll get killed.'

'Shh,' said Fatima, pushing me down into her lap. 'He's a rascal. I'll put him back when I return and he won't come to any harm. Now stop worrying.'

But I stared and stared at him until we had rounded the corner of the road and he and the house disappeared from view. I turned and looked at the others. They sat silently, their eyes fixed on the road ahead. No one seemed aware of my terrible anguish or how in that moment I suddenly knew with overwhelming certainty that something had irrevocably ended for us there and, like Rex's unfeigned, innocent affection, it would never return.

The short journey to the taxi depot in the Old City opposite the Damascus Gate passed without much incident. We were stopped again at the checkpoint outside the zone, and my father explained once more why we were leaving. When we reached the depot, we got out and transferred our luggage to a taxi which would take us to Damascus by way of Amman. To reach Damascus from Jerusalem, one would normally have taken the northern route through Ras al-Naqura. But all that part of Palestine was a raging battleground and no car could travel that way. Hence we had to take the longer and more roundabout route through Amman. The taxi depot was bustling with people leaving Palestine like us. There was a different atmosphere here to the one we had got used to in Qatamon. As it was a wholly Arab area, there was no sound of gun-fire and, though it was full of crowds of people crying and saying goodbye, it felt safe and familiar.

Fatima stood by the car which would take us away. For all her efforts at self-control, tears were coursing down her cheeks. She embraced and kissed the three of us in turn. My father said, 'Mind you look after the house until I come back,' and she nodded wordlessly. I clung desperately to the material of her kaftan but she gently disengaged my fingers. As we got into the taxi and the doors were shut, she drew up close and pressed her sad face against the window. We drove off, leaving her and Muhammad looking after us until they were no more than specks on the horizon, indistinguishable from the other village men and women who were there that day.

No doubt my parents thought they were sparing us pain by keeping our departure secret from us until the very last moment. They also believed we would be away for a short while only and so making a fuss of leaving Jerusalem was unnecessary. But in the event, they turned out to be woefully wrong. We never set eyes on Fatima or our dog or the city we had known ever again. Like a body prematurely buried, unmourned, without coffin or ceremony, our hasty, untidy exit from Jerusalem was no way to have said goodbye to our home, our country and all that we knew and loved.

I did not know until much later that, although my parents had accepted for some time that we would have to leave Jerusalem, if only for a while, there were two major events which had finally persuaded them to go. The first was the death of Abdul-Qadir al-Husseini and the second, close on its heels, was the massacre at Deir Yassin. In the first week of April, the battle to control the road to Jerusalem had raged between Jewish and Arab forces. Fighting was particularly fierce at the strategically important village of al-Qastal, ten kilometres to the west of Jerusalem. This was built on top of a hill and derived its name (castle) from an ancient fortress whose remains still stood there. It was there, as the Arab side was winning the battle (in which Husseini was joined by our Qatamon commander Abu Dayyeh and his unit), that he was killed by a Jewish soldier from the Palmach. This was a special unit of the Haganah whose men were highly trained for difficult or dangerous assignments. While Abdul-Qadir's death meant little to the Jews it had a profound impact on the Arab side. Even my father, who was sceptical about the Arab forces' chances of success, shared in the general hope embodied in Abdul-Qadir's courage and commitment. His death was therefore seen as an omen of impending disaster.

In the wake of his killing, it was said that the Arab fighters were so overwhelmed with grief that most of them escorted his body back to Jerusalem. This emotional send-off left al-Qastal unguarded and enabled the Jewish forces to regain it later that day. They were exultant and claimed that the Arab fighters were deserting in droves and returning to their villages. Traces of that triumphalism are still evident today. When I saw al-Qastal on a sad, windswept day in 1998, Israeli flags were fluttering from its old castle walls and placards declaring it to be the site of a major Israeli victory.

So great was people's shock and grief that Abdul-Qadir's funeral at the Dome of the Rock in the Old City on 7 April drew a crowd of 30,000 mourners.

Two days later, on 9 April, Irgun and Stern Gang gunmen perpetrated a massacre at Deir Yassin, a small village on the outskirts of Jerusalem. This was the unmentionable thing which Ziyad and I were not allowed to know. The people of Deir Yassin were mainly engaged in stone quarrying and had been peaceable throughout the troubles besetting other parts of Palestine. They had even concluded a non-aggression pact with the nearby Jewish settlement of Givat Sha'ul, approved by the Haganah, at the beginning of April 1948. The accounts of what the Jewish attackers had done to the villagers were truly shocking. The survivors who fled came with stories of mutilation, the rape of young girls and the murder of pregnant women and their babies. Some 250 people were massacred in cold blood (though recent estimates have put the number at between 100 and 200). Twenty of the men were driven in a lorry by the Irgun fighters and paraded in triumph around the streets of the Jewish areas of Jerusalem. They were then brought back and shot directly over the quarries in which they had been working and into which their bodies were thrown. The surviving villagers fled in terror, and the empty village was then occupied by Jewish forces.

The worst of it was that the gangs who had carried out the killings boasted about what they had done and threatened publicly to do so again. They said it had been a major success in clearing the Arabs out of their towns and villages. In this they were right, for news of the atrocity, disseminated by both the Jewish and the Arab media in Palestine and the surrounding Arab states, spread terror throughout the country. But because of Deir Yassin's proximity to Jerusalem, the news reached us first and led to an accelerated exodus from our city. The rest of the country was powerfully affected too. Menachem Begin, the leader of the Irgun, said with satisfaction that the massacre had helped in the conquest of places as far away as Tiberias and Haifa. He said it was worth half a dozen army battalions in the war against the Palestinian Arabs.

On 30 April, the Palmach unit of the Haganah launched a huge attack on the St Simon monastery. They overcame the contingent of Arab fighters inside and within twenty-four hours had taken control of the monastery. Fierce fighting ensued between them and the Arab battalions defending Qatamon for a full two days before it was brought to an end by the British army. Ibrahim Abu Dayyeh fought and was wounded in this final battle. A twenty-four-hour truce was agreed between the two sides, but before it ended the Jews had occupied the whole of Qatamon up to the boundary of the British zone. The Sakakini family had been the last to stay on, but on 30 April they too left their home. Throughout April, the Arab League was deliberating over plans of invasion to defend Palestine. These involved various combinations of Arab forces which would cross into Palestine from the neighbouring states and rescue the Palestinians. But none of them came to anything, while the Jews continued to consolidate their hold on the parts of the country they had conquered. In Jerusalem, they had control of most of the new city, which included our neighbourhood, while the Arabs retained the Old City.

We heard that Fatima kept going back to check on our house for as long as she could brave the journey. But in the end, it was too dangerous and she could go no longer. Her own village, al-Maliha, was conquered by the Jews (Israelis by then) in August 1948 and its people were made refugees. She escaped to the village of al-Bireh, east of Jerusalem and still in Arab hands, where we presume she stayed. After that news of her died out. In the chaos that attended the fall of Palestine and the mass exodus of its people, lives were wrenched apart, families brutally sundered, life-long friendships abruptly severed. No organisation existed to help people trace those they had lost.

And so it was that we too lost Fatima, not knowing how to pluck her from the human whirlpool that had swallowed her after our departure. As for Rex, whom we last saw that April morning in 1948, no news of him reached us ever again.

YAHYA YAKHLIF

The Hyena

The tunnel appears endless. The darkness is thick and heavy, and his feet move with difficulty. The darkness is hills and deep hollows, metaphor. The vision is clear. Heartbeats amplify, and the man imagines that he is seeing through the eye cavities of a skull. Suddenly a hyena emerged, all at once. Its fangs and claws protruded. He stopped. Stopped. His feet were nailed to the ground.

The hyena's eyes glow, evil oozes from them. The hyena moved, its panting sounds like snorts and turning into what sounds like wails.

He was devoured by fear and felt the fangs of terror ravaging him. He imagined the hyena would eat him without him being able to resist. The hyena advanced and lifted its tail with caution, then charged him instantly. It struck with its tail like an adder, whipping him with it.

The man felt the whip burn his face, and the hyena's urine flowing down his chin. The man had become a hyena, and lost consciousness. Then, the hyena walked through the tunnel with the man after it as he becomes immersed in imaginary water and called out in a dry and wounded voice: 'Father ... father ... wait for me.'

The man awoke from his sleep with panic painted on his face. His hand reached out searching and switched on the lights, bathing the room in dazzling brightness. He squinted his eyes and shook the woman sleeping next to him. The woman stirred. Disturbed by the light, she told him to switch it off as she buried her head in the blanket. He shook her violently feeling something trembling in his depths.

She opened her eyes. As her gaze fell upon his tired features, she shook her head and said, 'Was it the same dream?' He buried his face between his hands and continued burying it until it appeared to her as though he were whimpering. She reached for a box of cigarettes, lighting one for him and lifting his head as she fondled his cheeks. Then she planted the cigarette between his lips.

The cigarette quivered as the rings of smoke spread out. Their child cried in his room, so the wife got up and out of bed and walked towards the door. In the camp, their sounds were piercing, and various slogans were chanted in the area.

The beads of sweat accumulated on your brow, and the placards appeared and the angry grimacing faces. What's happening? And how?

The microphone is in your hand. Your throat is sore, as though the blade of a knife were touching it. There's an old lady chanting and chanting. What do they want? They all reject what you're saying. Your lips move. The microphone crackles and in your head a wobbly fan rotates. You look like a factory owner confronting a strike. Your lips move. The microphone crackles, the faces are red and their blood is boiling, anger overwhelms you, it spreads like fire. There's a confrontation. You turn around, and then suddenly, there's a deluge.

He anxiously stubbed out the cigarette and once again buried his face in his hands.

'There must be a reckoning.'

'We must crush them.'

'They're a mob.'

He was the only honest one, that brave boy who was injured

in his leg at the Cola roundabout in the May battles. He said with agitation: 'When we raise a slogan that divides the masses, then that slogan must be untrue.' (You couldn't control yourself, you yelled at him, so he turned around and left).

The wife returned and told him that she covered the child well. Then she said some other things, and then she stretched and yawned and descended into a deep sleep.

He closed his eyes.

The hyena began to run across the flat earth. And the hyena-man runs and pants, and occasionally he'd call as loudly as he could: 'Wait for me ... wait for me ... father ... father ...' His throat had become dry and he could only swallow with difficulty.

Amidst the darkness and haze, he could see the hyena as a black heap rolling around up high. The flat ground ended, and the hyena started scaling an incline. The man climbs behind it as small rocks fall below his feet. From time to time the hyena stops briefly, but as soon as the man nears, it continues climbing.

Finally, the hyena reaches its cave with its low door. It stands at the door. Its breath is hot, its fangs protruding. Its eyes are glowing red coals being blown by the fierce winds. The man nears as he calls with a wounded voice 'father ... father ... wait.' Like a spooked horse he charges towards the cave, hitting his forehead against its ceiling.

The man awoke from his sleep screaming. He threw the blankets off himself and turned on the lights. He saw the wardrobe and his sleeping wife and the picture hanging on the wall. The child cried in the next room. His wife awoke from her sleep and rubbed her eyes, then looked at the man and gasped in horror. A line of blood was trickling down his forehead.

Translated by Joseph R. Farag

IBRAHIM NASRALLAH

Excerpt from Street Olives

All we had left was the night.

'With a little daring you could say she was one of the most imposing people I ever saw in my life, and I'm not saying that just because I'm Salwa.'

She was talking about her friend Zeinab.

'She was so impressive – her simplicity, her physique and her accent, which was dotted with elements of Palestinian dialect. There was that sparkle in her eyes and her confidence that she had the right to ask difficult questions that were painful to answer, and that maybe didn't have answers.

'She used to say, "I sometimes wonder if I might have been less homesick among my own people. Sometimes I ask myself what it was that I lost there in Palestine that meant that I feel like a refugee living here, a few hours away from my homeland and my family? Sometimes I think I can go back to them, and to my childhood memories, that I can relive those memories and live other memories that I didn't live. But I feel that something was snatched away from me there in Palestine. Could I call it my life? Could I call it a spiritual choice to be the person I wanted to be and as every cell inside me wanted?"'

* * *

I'm Zeinab. I look at myself now and it never occurs to me, not for a moment, that I took a wrong turn. I look at the people around me trying to draw conclusions about me, as if they were deciding my fate.

Whenever you became part of your idea, they said you were about to go mad, but when you become that idea, you're madness itself! Isn't that right? It's as if there's a margin of safety between you and yourself and if you cross it you lose everything.

Anyway, there I was, stuffing my belongings into a small bag, crying and laughing at the same time, though I still couldn't see the real reason for either crying or laughing.

And when I told Alaeddin I had to take the books he said, 'I can't say no to that.'

He came into the room behind me, and when I started taking the books down off the shelf, he laughed and said, 'We have this book at home, and this one, and this one'.

I couldn't believe that two libraries – one here in the Sabaa Bahrat district of Damascus and the other near Acre – could be twins in this way.

'You're joking,' I told him.

'No, I'm not joking, I swear.'

The truth was simple but beautiful: it was just that these books were part of a widely sold series, but I saw the discovery as a good omen.

* * *

The local people were fretful. Alaeddin was late. Had something bad happened to him, God forbid? Had they caught him on the road? Should we send someone to look for him?

They knew where to obtain weapons, and Hajj Abdel Hamid, an old friend of the revolution, had often fought with them. 'Hajj, you take a rest, your age isn't working in your favour,' they begged him.

And he would embarrass them, saying: 'Admit it, you're fed up with me. I'm now a burden on you.'

'No, really. Go home, fetch your family and come, then go into town the way you want and choose whichever house you like.'

'Listen, I still have some strength in me and it would be a shame to waste it somewhere else, on another mission less noble than this one.'

But he finally admitted he was too old. That was when he was unable to pull out of a skirmish and some of the young fighters had to stay with him.

'You pull back. I'll stay,' he said.

'No way.'

British weapons were constantly pouring into the hands of the Zionists, and it looked like the whole situation was moving in a different direction from the direction it had been moving in the long term. The battles were fiercer, even the small ones.

They were surrounded for a whole day and saw death roaming the hills, its dark shadow closing in on them, but they kept fighting. They felt that every bullet they fired was a part of their souls, that with every bullet death took a step towards them, since they were so short of bullets.

* * *

'You'll be in charge of obtaining weapons for us in Damascus,' they told him.

* * *

I loved him as soon as I saw him. I went out to open the gate, and that day all the doors in my heart were opened.

'Say to your father, "He's coming, and the palm tree's coming with him!"'

'What?'

'The palm tree.'

There weren't any palm trees with him, either in front of him, behind him or on either side.

'I don't understand!' I said.

'As I said, tell the hajj, "He's coming and the palm tree's coming with him."'

Maybe he's the palm tree, I thought. He was tall and handsome in his black suit and his red fez.

'Who is it, Zeinab?' my father said from across the courtyard as I stood hesitant at the gate.

'Who is it?' he asked again.

In confusion, I said, 'He's coming, and the palm tree's coming with him.'

'Let it in. Let him in quickly,' he said impatiently.

Then I realised what a mistake I had made when I kept him waiting there at the gate.

My father stared at him and shouted with joy like a child: 'Alaeddin? My God, now you're a man.'

* * *

'Where's Zeinab in this?' Salwa shouted in Abdel Rahman's face.

'Where is she?' she added, tapping the manuscript with her fist.

'All I can see here is her ghost. We all turned into ghosts when you wrote about us. We were human beings. Do you know what it means to be human beings? Of flesh and blood and soul?'

* * *

We had spent long nights together, me and Zeinab, enough for us to go over our stories thousands of times. We didn't really have anything but those nights.

* * *

Abdel Hamid told me later that he had a special affection for this young man because he was the smartest little devil he'd seen in his life and had shown exceptional daring when he had managed to smuggle two pistols and a bomb to the revolutionaries in Acre jail, which enabled them to escape after they threatened the guards with them. That was Alaeddin, Zeinab.

'And I loved him more,' Zeinab told me. 'And I would have loved him even more if Palestine hadn't turned into a piece of meat, chewed over by everyone who had teeth, as is happening now. Palestine used to be an intrinsic part of people's honour. You know what, Salwa? Mankind has been given long enough to prove it has a conscience on the question of Palestine, but unfortunately so far it's proved that it doesn't have a conscience.

'As for me, I've kept wondering whether I really loved him or whether I was answering a mysterious call from that country that he comes from. At the time no one thought twice when they heard the call – "Your brothers are on such-and-such hill, surrounded and seeking help," for example. People would throw down whatever they were holding and set off without looking back. The call for freedom was stronger than the call for bread, more beautiful than children, wives, jobs or the warmth of home.'

* * *

'Is there anything else you want to take with you, Alaeddin?' my father asked.

Alaeddin didn't know what to say. He always took his time.

'We can get the guns ready tomorrow or the day after. I also want to see your city,' he said.

And yet he wouldn't leave our house!

'How can you see our city when you're stuck between four walls? You've left it too late. You have to get ready to go back tomorrow,' said Abdel Hamid.

'But, uncle, I haven't seen it yet.'

'Don't worry, you'll see it often.'

Alaeddin didn't have anything else to say.

'Zeinab,' said Abdel Hamid.

'Yes, father.'

'Get ready to go with Alaeddin tomorrow, and tonight we'll sign the engagement agreement.'

'Father!' I jumped for joy.

'I'm your guardian too and I can marry you off too, at my whim!' he said to Alaeddin.

'Uncle!'

'Try another one. We knew those tricks before you were born. Have you forgotten that I was a young man too once?' said Abdel Hamid.

* * *

I cried when I said goodbye to my mother, my father and my sisters. I didn't know why I cried. Was it because I was happy to be going with him, or because I was happy I would finally see Palestine – a country I had never thought was far enough away for me to say that going there meant being apart from my family.

'My mother called me Alaeddin because she loved the stories about him in the *Thousand and One Nights*,' he told me on the way.

* * *

'They completely ignored their anxieties. When they saw me with him they forgot they had sent him to fetch guns, and the whole town gathered around me.'

'Alaeddin, what's the story?' they asked him.

'She's my wife,' he said, pointing at me.

There was a stunned silence.

'Zeinab, Hajj Abdel Hamid's daughter,' he added.

'Hajj Abdel Hamid's daughter!' they said.

I hadn't realised till then how much they respected my father. Dozens of people jostled to kiss me, incessantly and incredulously. 'Hajj Abdel Hamid's daughter, welcome!' they intoned.

I've never been as loved as I was at that moment. Even Alaeddin's love didn't compare with that love. I thought that meeting him was the most beautiful moment in my life. No, it was the most beautiful moment in my life until Ayman appeared in the world. Then I looked back and saw all my time there and whispered in Ayman's ear: 'You're my hope.' Ayman that I almost lost on that fateful night when I crawled across the terrain looking for Alaeddin.

* * *

At sunset that day Alaeddin's horse turned up, alone and sad. It lingered at the door before neighing. It stamped on the evening with its hoofs and fretted.

I knew what it meant: it was the only creature that dared bring me the news. It kept neighing and crying in anguish until I climbed on its back.

'Where to, Zeinab?'

Two streams of tears on the horse's face, and two more on Zeinab's face.

It galloped and galloped into the darkness in front of it, away from the darkness behind it. And suddenly it stopped.

'Who goes there?' I heard the men shouting, and dismounted.

'It's Zeinab.'

'What brings you here?'

They were angry.

'Where's Alaeddin?' I asked.

They didn't say anything.

For three days the country had been following the battle of the bridge. Sometimes the local men would win it back, sometimes the Stern Gang would hold it. Neither side wanted to destroy it because they both had an interest in leaving it standing.

After three days the bridge stood in the middle, not in the hands of this side or that side. The local Palestinians had been forced to retreat and had left Alaeddin under the bridge.

'I'll fetch him,' I told them.

'What are you talking about? If we make any movement tonight, they could easily hear it on the other side. That's why they're watching him. Wait till the morning and you'll see with your own eyes. If we could get to him we wouldn't have left him there.'

They never forgot that I was Hajj Abdel Hamid's daughter. When they were talking with me, I felt they were talking with him, because there was part of him in me.

'The horse gave us the slip. It set off in that direction at a gallop,' one of them said.

'Suddenly the gates of hell opened and bullets lit up the hills. Shells exploded, with flashes of fire in the black of the night. Then the silhouette of a prancing horse emerged from the darkness. And then we saw the horse going back.'

'Did it reach him?' I asked.

'We don't know, but the horse looked even more agitated when it came past us and disappeared into the night behind us.'

* * *

Under a sad sun, between two hills of burnt rock, naked to the barrels of the rifles, stood the bridge.

Zeinab stayed far back, behind the hill, and stayed there in silence with the horse until night fell again. Then she took the horse by the halter, tied it to a bramble bush and sneaked forward alone.

She felt around on the ground for a long time, looking for his body, looking for his face, for the eyes through which he had looked at her, for his hands.

Suddenly she found him right in front of her, just a dead body.

'I wanted to scream, but I couldn't. They would have killed him again and I was stunned, as if I'd never seen death in battle before. I started dragging his body away from the bridge but then the gates of hell opened up over my head.

'I had to scream, and I started to scream, not out of fear but because I wanted to scream. The bullets died down and I calmed down. I was surprised to find myself lying on top of his body, protecting him from the bullets – the bullets that will keep echoing in my ears for the rest of my life.

'Then I went back to dragging him until we reached the bush. I put him on his horse and brought him back. The sun was rising, so far behind me that I thought it would never reach me. I thought it would never reach the middle of the sky. And when they set about taking him down off the horse, I was in another world. But something inside me brought me to my senses again and I screamed and cried as if he had been killed a second time.

'One of his hands had been cut off at the wrist, and now it was missing.'

* * *

'We're going to bury him,' one of them said.

'No,' I shouted. 'We're not going to bury him till I find his hand. I'm not going to bury him.'

'Be reasonable, Zeinab.'

'I won't bury him,' I said.

I fainted close to him, and when I came round I found my hands gripping his arm.

Later they said they tried to bury him but they couldn't free his arm from my fingers without breaking the fingers.

So Alaeddin was in two parts, each in a different place.

With Zeinab between the two, with his horse.

In the evening she went back to the hill where the men were still posted, and behind her in the distance his mother followed her.

The men said, 'We'll go and fetch his hand.'

'If anyone has to die for his hand, then it's going to be me,' said Zeinab.

Zeinab ended up scrambling again across the rough terrain, with bloody fingers, cuts on her feet and a broken heart, until she reached the place. She groped around on the ground and cried.

'What if they took it with them to prove they'd killed him? It wouldn't be the first time they've done that,' she thought to herself.

His hand should be here, she said to herself, and she rushed around searching for it frantically.

'And finally, my fingers found it, my blind fingers. I trembled and cried and wanted to scream. I wanted to die right there. I wanted his warm hand back, a hand quite different from this cold hand. I wanted his hand as it was when it knew me, the hand that knew my hand, that knew my shoulders, my hair, the hand that waved at me, his playful, lithe hand. I wanted to scream, 'Where is it?' but I was worried they might bury him without this hand that didn't remember me, this hand that used to remember me, this hesitant hand that took comfort in me and liked to bury itself in my breast. I had to find it. Otherwise I would have spent the rest of my life looking for it.'

'Did you find it?'

'For heaven's sake, auntie!'

I cried and my hand reached into my breast to take it out.

And we went back.

Two women and a horse,

And three broken hearts.

'Leave us with him,' his mother said, cradling his head between her knees.

His horse was restive in the courtyard.

Zeinab shouted, 'Let that one in.'

They looked out of the door. 'Who?'

'His horse.'

'His horse!'

'You've heard, haven't you?' his mother shouted.

The horse came in – the horse that lay down beside him, its neck and face pressed against the ground, calm and crying.

* * *

With trembling hands and tearful eyes that rolled, Zeinab began to sew his hand back on.

'Give me the needle, my girl,' said Alaeddin's mother.

His mother turned his head and put it on Zeinab's knee and her hands began to work – hands she felt she was seeing for the first time, frail hands, like hands that had never planted a tree.

Her face was covered in tears. She stopped, wiped her face with the edge of her sleeve and continued.

They stayed the whole night

Till dawn broke.

The men knocked on the door, and came in timidly.

'Now you can bury him,' Zeinab said.

'Come on, lift him up,' said his mother.

They walked off, and his horse walked in the funeral procession too.

Translated by Jonathan Wright

Settlement

Here a tree blossomed
Here a sparrow wandered
Here a violin was lost to nostalgia
Here a star loved a little girl
Here a nightingale stole fruit!
Here a boy wrote a book of songs
for someone else in his neighbourhood who loved
Here there was a field of pears
Here a student memorised the lesson to the point of exhaustion
Here there was merry laughter
and the talk of sunset with swallows
before a tank rolled over
bullying its way towards the hilltop
To build for the army of invaders,
over my mother's bosom, a settlement.

Translated by Atef Alshaer

ELIAS KHOURY

Excerpt from Gate of the Sun

How am I supposed to talk to you or with you or about you?

HEY, YOU!

How am I supposed to talk to you or with you or about you?

Should I tell you stories you already know, or be silent and let you go wherever it is you go? I come close to you, walking on tiptoe so as not to wake you, and then I laugh at myself because all I want is to wake you. I need one thing – one thing, dear God: that this man drowning in his own eyes should get up, open his eyes and say something.

But I'm lying.

Did you know you've turned me into a liar?

I say I want one thing, but I want thousands of things. I lie, God take pity on you, on me and on your poor mother. Yes, we forgot your mother. You told me all your stories, and you never told me how your mother died. You told about the death of your blind father and how you slipped into Galilee and attended his funeral. You stood on the hill above the village of Deir al-Asad, seeing but unseen, weeping but not weeping.

At the time I believed you. I believed that intuition had led you there to your house, hours before he died. But now I don't.

At the time I was bewitched by your story. Now the spell is broken, and I no longer believe you.

But your mother?

Why didn't you say anything about her death?

Is your mother dead?

Do you remember the story of the icon of the Virgin Mary?

We were living through the civil war in Lebanon, and you were saying that war shouldn't be like that. You even advised me, when I came back from Beijing as a doctor, not to take part in the war and asked me to go with you to Palestine.

'But Yunes, you don't go to fight. You go because of your wife.'

You gave me a long lecture about the meaning of war and then said something about the picture of the Virgin Mary in your house, and that was when I asked you if your mother was Christian and how the sheikh of the village of Ain al-Zaitoun could have married a Christian woman. You explained that she wasn't a Christian but loved the Virgin and used to put her picture under her pillow. She'd made you love the Virgin, too, because she was the mistress of all the world's women and because her picture was beautiful – a woman bending her head over her son, born swaddled in his shroud.

'And what did the sheikh think?' I asked you.

It was then that you explained to me that your father, the sheikh, was blind, and that he never saw the picture at all.

When did Nahilah tell you of your mother's death?

Why don't you tell me? Is it because your wife said your mother had asked to be buried with the picture and this caused a problem in the village?

Why do you sleep like that and not answer?

You sleep like sleep itself. You sleep in sleep, and are drowning. The doctor said you had a blood clot in the brain, were clinically dead, and there was no hope. I refused to believe him.

I see you before me and can do nothing.

I hold conversations with you and tell you stories. I'll tell you everything. What do you say – I'll make tea, and we'll sit on the low chairs in front of your house and tell tales! You used to laugh at me because I don't smoke. You used to smoke your cigarette right to the end, chewing on the butt hanging between your lips and sucking in the smoke.

Now here I am. I close the door of your room. I sit next to you. I light a cigarette, draw the smoke deep into my lungs, and I tell you tales. And you don't answer.

The tea's gone cold, and I'm tired. You're immersed in your breathing and don't care.

Please don't believe them.

Do you remember the day when you came to me and say that everyone was sick of you, and I couldn't dispel the sadness from your round pale face? What was I supposed to say? Should I have said your day had passed, or hadn't yet come? You'd have been even more upset. I couldn't lie to you. So I'm sad too, and my sadness is a deep breach in my soul that I can't repair, but I swear I don't want you to die.

Why did you lie to me?

Why did you tell me after the mourners had left that Nahilah's death didn't matter, because a woman only dies if her man stops loving her, and Nahilah hadn't died because you still loved her?

'She's here,' you said, and you pointed at your eyes, wide open to show their dark grey. I was never able to identify the colour of your eyes – when I asked you, you would say that Nahilah didn't know what colour they were either, and that at Bab al-Shams she used to ask you about the colours of things.

You lied to me.

You convinced me that Nahilah hadn't died, and didn't finish the sentence. At the time I didn't take in what you'd said; I thought they were the beautiful words an old lover uses to heal his love. But death was in the other half of the sentence, because a man dies when his woman stops loving him, and you're dying because Nahilah stopped loving you when she died.

So here you are, drowsing.

Dear God, what drowsiness is this? And why do I feel a deathly drowsiness when I'm near you? I lie back in the chair and sleep. And when I get up in the middle of the night, I feel pain all over my body.

I come close to you, I see the air rolling around you, and I see that place I have not visited. I'd decided to go; everyone goes, so why not me? I'd go and have a look. I'd go and anchor the landmarks in my eyes. You used to tell me that you knew the sites because they were engraved on your eyes like indelible landmarks.

Translated by Humphrey Davies

GHASSAN ZAQTAN

Remembering the Grandmother

Pretexts come with her absence
and with the waiting of boats between
noon and afternoon
when the light is deeply fissured
and the satisfied prisoners, our grandmothers
in the plains, comb the sleep of hills
then age in their fissured sleep
We haven't seen the sea
but we can be certain, after the rosary prayers,
it's behind the line of hills,
says the girl who sweeps the courtyard

When I remembered
... when we had come up to the lighthouse
you lit a fire and kept me warm.

Beyond That

I have a wish to see the land
a wish to retrieve recitation from the wisdom of lectors
and to think like a falcon
I have a wish to see the land whole
return song to poetry,

call strange mountains my brothers
and release my heart from the corpse of longing
and from the thick honey of prophets

Four Sisters From Zakariya

Four sisters climb the mountain,
alone,
dressed in black
Four sisters
sigh
in front of the forest
Four sisters
are reading
tear-stained mail
– A train shunted through
the picture
of the settlement of Artov
– A horse
carried a girl
from our village, Zakariya
The horse whinnied
as it stood on the hill
behind the plain
Clouds
drifted lazily
over the ditch
Four sisters from Zakariya
are stood on the hill,
alone, dressed in black

Beirut, August 1982

How I wish he had not died
in last Wednesday's raid
as he strolled through Nazlat al-Bir –
my friend with blond hair,
as blond as a native of the wetlands of Iraq.
Like a woman held spellbound at her loom,
all summer long the war was weaving its warp and weft.
And that song, O Beiruuuuut!,
sang from every single radio
in my father's house in Al-Karama –
and probably in our old house in Beit Jala
(which, whenever I try to find it in the maze of the camp,
refuses to be found).
That song sang of what we knew –
it sang of our streets, narrow and neglected,
our people cheek by jowl in the slums made by war.
But the song did not sing about that summer in Beirut,
it did not tell us what was coming –
aeroplanes, bombardment, annihilation ...
The song was singing while my friend from Iraq –
who'd thought I was Moroccan from the countryside there –
limped bleeding to his death ...
His blond hair will never fade,
a beam of light seared into memory.

A Picture of the House in Beit Jala

He has to return to shut that window,
it isn't entirely clear
whether this is what he must do,
things are no longer clear
since he has lost them,
and it seems a hole somewhere within him
has opened up

Closing up the cracks has exhausted him
mending the fences
wiping the glass
cleaning the edges
and watching the dust that seems, since he has lost the things,
to lure his memories into hoax and ruse.
And from here his childhood appears as if it were a trick!
inspecting the doors has fully exhausted him
the window latches
the condition of the plants
and wiping the dust
that has not ceased flowing
into the rooms, on the beds, sheets, pots
and on the picture frames on the walls

Since he has lost them he stays with friends
who become fewer
sleeps in their beds
that become narrower
while the dust gnaws at his memories 'there'

... he must return to shut that window

the upper story window which he often forgets
at the end of the stairway that leads to the roof

Since he has lost them
he aimlessly walks
and the day's small
purposes are also no longer clear

All translated by Fady Joudah

NAOMI SHIHAB NYE

Different Ways to Pray

There was the method of kneeling,
a fine method, if you lived in a country
where stones were smooth.
The women dreamed wistfully of bleached courtyards,
hidden corners where knee fit rock.
Their prayers were weathered rib bones,
small calcium words uttered in sequence,
as if this shedding of syllables could somehow
fuse them to the sky.
There were the men who had been shepherds so long
they walked like sheep.
Under the olive trees, they raised their arms –
Hear us! We have pain on earth!
We have so much pain there is no place to store it!
But the olives bobbed peacefully
in fragrant buckets of vinegar and thyme.
At night the men ate heartily, flat bread and white cheese,
and were happy in spite of the pain,
because there was also happiness.
Some prized the pilgrimage,
wrapping themselves in new white linen
to ride buses across miles of vacant sand.
When they arrived at Mecca
they would circle the holy places,

on foot, many times,
they would bend to kiss the earth
and return, their lean faces housing mystery.
While for certain cousins and grandmothers
the pilgrimage occurred daily,
lugging water from the spring
or balancing the baskets of grapes.
These were the ones present at births,
humming quietly to perspiring mothers.
The ones stitching intricate needlework into children's dresses,
forgetting how easily children soil clothes.
There were those who didn't care about praying.
The young ones. The ones who had been to America.
They told the old ones, you are wasting your time.
Time? – The old ones prayed for the young ones.
They prayed for Allah to mend their brains,
for the twig, the round moon,
to speak suddenly in a commanding tone.
And occasionally there would be one
who did none of this,
the old man Fowzi, for example, Fowzi the fool,
who beat everyone at dominoes,
insisted he spoke with God as he spoke with goats,
and was famous for his laugh.

Blood

'A true Arab knows how to catch a fly in his hands,'
my father would say. And he'd prove it,
cupping the buzzer instantly
while the host with the swatter stared.

In the spring our palms peeled like snakes.
True Arabs believed watermelon could heal fifty ways.
I changed these to fit the occasion.

Years before, a girl knocked,
wanted to see the Arab.
I said we didn't have one.
After that, my father told me who he was,
'Shihab' – 'shooting star' –
a good name, borrowed from the sky.
Once I said, 'When we die, we give it back?'
He said that's what a true Arab would say.

Today the headlines clot in my blood.
A little Palestinian dangles a truck on the front page.
Homeless fig, this tragedy with a terrible root
is too big for us. What flag can we wave?
I wave the flag of stone and seed,
table mat stitched in blue.

I call my father, we talk around the news.
It is too much for him,
neither of his two languages can reach it.
I drive into the country to find sheep, cows,
to plead with the air:

Who calls anyone *civilised*?
Where can the crying heart graze?
What does a true Arab do now?

Everything in Our World Did Not Seem to Fit

Once they started invading us.
Taking our houses and trees, drawing lines,
pushing us into tiny places.
It wasn't a bargain or deal or even a real war.
To this day they pretend it was.
But it was something else.
We were sorry what happened to them but
we had nothing to do with it.
You don't think what a little plot of land means
till someone takes it and you can't go back.
Your feet still want to walk there.
Now you are drifting worse
than homeless dust, very lost feeling.
I cried even to think of our hallway,
cool stone passage inside the door.
Nothing would fit for years.
They came with guns, uniforms, declarations.
LIFE magazine said,
'It was surprising to find some Arabs still in their houses.'
Surprising? Where else would we be?
Up in the hillsides?
Conversing with mint and sheep, digging in dirt?
Why was someone else's need for a home
greater than our own need for our own homes
we were already living in? No one has ever been able

to explain this sufficiently. But they find
a lot of other things to talk about.

How Palestinians Keep Warm

Choose one word and say it over
and over, till it builds a fire inside your mouth.
Adhafera, the one who holds out, Alphard, solitary one,
the stars were named by people like us.
Each night they line up on the long path between worlds.
They nod and blink, no right or wrong
in their yellow eyes. Dirah, little house,
unfold your walls and take us in.

My well went dry, my grandfather's grapes
have stopped singing. I stir the coals,
my babies cry. How will I teach them
they belong to the stars?
They build forts of white stone and say, 'This is mine'.
How will I teach them to love Mizar, veil, cloak,
to know that behind it an ancient man
is fanning a flame?
He stirs the dark wind of our breath.
He says the veil will rise
till they see us shining, spreading like embers
on the blessed hills.

Well, I made that up. I'm not so sure about Mizar.
But I know we need to keep warm here on earth
And when your shawl is as thin as mine is, you tell stories.

NATHALIE HANDAL

Echoes: A Historical Afterward

The reason is they've been killed
The truth you've been too
The truth is you are now without a home
The reason is they're in your home
The reason is they've convinced themselves you left
The truth is you only went to safety
The truth is they never let you back
The reason is they needed to protect their tribe
The truth is you are part of the same tribe
But no one speaks about that
The reason is it's easier to be a threat
How else can they justify the killing.

Here

The Old Port of Jaffa
Is here
The sunlight poised
On our memories
Here
The old stone houses
With our tiles tiles tiles
Evidence of homes buried
In different names
Here
The years we never defined
Here
The echoes we collected
In each other
Here
The shivering breeze
Against our skin
The dark paradise
Under our eyes
Here
But you were not here
And I was not here
They say
But we were here
We are here
We are here.

The Oranges

They were all around me
but grew heavier and heavier
until I couldn't carry them
anymore –
who can live with such weight
around the heart
who can carry a bent flame
across the night
where pieces of a moon
keep trying to declare something
to each other
but never do
who can see anything
when light is displaced
when the oranges have been taken
far away from where they belong
To Sami, Jaffa
when you don't touch me
it's your noise that blows open
my darkness
and maybe, I ask
(but never ask you)
the hole you fell into
is nothing
it's what remains around it
that matters
But even in love
war inhabits me

Gaza City

I sit in a grey room on a bed with a grey blanket
and wait for the muezzin to stand up.
The chants enter my window and I think of all
those men and women bowing in prayer, fear escaping
them at every stroke, a new sadness entering
their spirit as their children line up in the streets
like prisoners in a death camp.
I walk towards the broken window
my head slightly slanted and try to catch a glimpse
of the city of spirits – those killed
who pass through the narrow opening of their tombs.
My hands and the side of my right face
against the cold wall, I hide like a slut, ashamed.
I pull the collar of my light blue robe so hard
it tears, one side hanging as everyone's lives hang here.
My fingers sink deep into my flesh,
I scratch myself, three lines scar my chests,
three faiths pound in my head and I wonder
if God is buried in the rubble. Every house is a prison,
every room a dog cage. Debke is no longer part of life,
only funerals are. Gaza is pregnant
with people and no one helps with the labour.
There are no streets, no hospitals, no schools,
no airport, no air to breathe.
And here I am in a room behind a window,
helpless, useless.
In America, I would be watching television
listening to CNN saying the Israelis demand,
terrorism must stop. Here all I see is inflicted terror,
children who no longer know they are children.

Milosevic is put on trail, but what about Sharon?
I finally get dressed, stand directly in front of the window
and choke on my spit as the gun shots start,
the F16 fighter jets pass in their daily routine.

Jenin

A night without a blanket, a blanket
belonging to someone else, someone
else living in our homes.
All I want is the quietness of blame to leave,
the words from dying tongues to fall,
all I want is to see a row of olive trees,
a field of tulips, to forget
the maze of intestines, the dried corners
of a soldier's mouth, all I want is for
the small black-eyed child to stop
wondering when the fever will stop
the noise will stop, all I want is
a loaf of bread, some water
and help for the stranger's torn arm,
all I want is what we have inherited
from the doves, a perfect line of white,
but a question still haunts me at night:
where are the bodies?

Bethlehem

Secrets live in the space between our footsteps.
The words of my grandfather echoed in my dreams,
as the years kept his beads and town.
I saw Bethlehem, all in dust, an empty town
with a torn piece of newspaper lost in its narrow streets.
Where could everyone be? Graffiti and stones answered.
And where was the real Bethlehem – the one my grandfather came from?
Handkerchiefs dried the pain from my hands. Olive trees and tears continued to remember.
I walked the town until I reached an old Arab man dressed in a white robe.
I stopped him and asked, 'Aren't you the man I saw in my grandfather's stories?'
He looked at me and left. I followed him – asked him why he left?
He continued walking. I stopped, turned around and realised
he had left me the secrets in the space between his footsteps.

SHARIF S. ELMUSA

Flawed Landscape

And it came to pass,
We lost the war; and became a nation of refugees.
It is always the beginning.
Fuelled by fear; my father gathered
The clan, lugged me in his arms,
And headed, on his peasant feet,
Across plain and impassable mountain,
Without a compass, headed east.

We set down in a camp in a desert,
Without the sinuous sands of the movies,
By the gateless town of Jericho.
In that flawed landscape,
Under the shadow of the dark rocks
Of the Mount of Temptation,
The world was kind to us.
The United Nations, our godfather;
Doled out flour and rice and cheddar;
'yellow', cheese – sharp beyond our palettes.

My father remembered his twelve olive trees
Every day for ten years. He remembered
The peasants saying to the olive tree,
Had she felt for their toil,

She'd yield not olives, but tears,
And the tree answering,
Tears you have enough; I give you oil
To light your lamps, to nourish, and to heal.

Then one day he let go. Let go.
My father was no Ulysses.
He found a new land, and stayed away
On the farm, eking out some rough happiness.

My mother stayed home.
Shepherded a pack of twelve, cleaned and yelled
And, for punishment, summoned father's shadow.
She stuffed our thin bones with sentiments,
As if to make us immobile.

Her past was insatiable:
The new house they had just built,
Windows on four sides, tall and arched,
To let in the ample light,
To spread out the prayers;
How my father rushed to ask for her hand
The day after she had kept him in line
At the water well; how they found
The body of her brother soaked
In sweet-scented blood,
At the police station,
After he had been killed by the discriminate bullets
Of the British soldiers.

No statues were built in the camp;
The dead would have been ashamed.

The living dreamed – the dreams of the wounded.
In their houses the radio was the hearth,
And the news of the oracle.

In the Refugee Camp

The huts were made of mud and hay,
Their thin roofs feared the rains,
And walls slouched like humbled me.
The streets were laid out in a grid,
As in New York,
But without the dignity of names
Or asphalt. Dust reigned.
Women grew pale
Chickens and children
Feeding them fables from the lost land.
And a madman sawed the minaret
Where a melodious voice
Cried for help on behalf of the believers.

Of course I gazed at the sky
On clear nights,
At stars drizzling
Soft grains of light,
At the moon's deliberate face,
At the good angel wrapped in purple air:
I had no holder
And nothing from heaven fell
In my crescent hands.
Ah, how I cursed Adam and Eve
And the one who made them refugees.

LIANA BADR

One Sky

He was standing at the side of the road, atop a pile of gravel, between the asphalt and the rocky mountainside. Frozen in place, with a fixed gaze, like a wax doll, his black eye gleaming at me. His serious stance, like a miniature knight on a chess board, caught my eye. I bent over and picked him up as if he were a piece of carbonised sand. His other eye appeared to be closed. The eyelid was swollen, covering it. Between his eyes was a red scar, evidence of a blow, below which his feathers had been plucked out.

His injury suggested that a predator had pecked him between his eyes but had not succeeded in killing him. One of our group speculated that a passing car had hit the reckless bird, being unable to avoid it, as birds do not recognise potential danger posed by moving vehicles. Another commented that a bird of prey must have attacked him to inflict such a severe injury.

I picked him up immediately and wrapped him in the white, silky shawl that still retained a blue mark in the form of the gold brooch that fastens the fabric of the traditional Tunisian sefseri cloak. I thanked God that the changeable spring weather had compelled me to bring what I had wrapped around my neck, so that I could use it to lift the injured bird from the dust without causing it to panic.

Cradling the small bird, I resumed walking towards the grassy slope, above which a patch of blue sky appeared. I hugged him close to my chest, hoping that the beating of my heart would transmit some warmth into his tiny, exhausted body. It seemed to me that the bird's fragility in the face of the random blows was at odds with the strength of his wings that carried him above the laws of earthly gravity. How much stronger than us he was, and yet immeasurably more fragile!

We carried on towards the slope. Above us shone the fresh spring sky, the brightness of which we had not known since the cold days of winter.

We proceed at a vigorous pace, leaving behind us a temporary construction for the curfew, following a month and a half of confinement by the tanks and armoured vehicles that had devastated the city. The soles of our feet enjoy the feel of the solid earth despite the large amount of gravel scattered on it. The features of our faces relax, after having stiffened from compulsory listening to the babble of the political programmes on the satellite television stations, which discuss our situation in a style no different from the entertainment programmes.

Our senses are shaken by the noise of the loudspeakers fixed to the Israeli Jeeps, which multiply around us like dangerous viruses as they recite their orders at us. We walk with all our determination, escaping, albeit temporarily, from the smells of poisonous gas bombs, and the garbage and waste, which has not been collected because of the curfew. Attempting to flee, if only for a moment, from our houses that have become our prisons. Expending most of our energy through our steps placed in the direction of the open air, so that we might forget how many incessant announcements are repeated around us at all hours of the night or day. Trying to ensure that, despite everything, our fundamental dreams of a different life are not shaken from our souls. As if that excursion of ours were no more than a break from all the instructions and orders that have been instilled in us and imposed upon us, like cages of chain mail.

Merely perhaps ... in order that we peek out between the solid bars of our prison, between one prohibition and another, at another blue patch of the sky of Palestine.

A sky that looks down on mountainous lands encircled by the ancient dry-stone walls that have prevented the earth from crumbling and collapsing since the times of the Romans and Phoenicians. A vast expanse, and over its hills spread the stone huts, like miniature fortresses, their rough stones forming houses to protect the crops and sheep of farmers since times long past, and forgotten by subsequent generations.

Under the shadows of the clouds, ceaselessly wandering above the eternally recurring summits, emerge from time to time the fortifications of Israeli military positions surrounded by barbed wire, ready to assume their roles in the conversion of our agricultural land into colonial settlements.

Looking from the West, these occupation positions surrounded by searchlights and barbed wire, with their immoral nature, are bathed in the splendour transmitted by these hills over which advance infinite clusters of olive trees. Converging in turn with the streamlined peaks stretching to the distant sea. Above its bright, shimmering waters another sky gently touches that iridescent, red copper twilight of the evening.

A sea, whose shimmering shadows we only glimpse from afar, because it remains hidden in the direction of the beach, which we are forbidden from reaching. Yet we never tire of gazing towards it whenever possible, making walking to it evidence of nostalgia. We use as a pretext the search for the flowers which the desert bears at this time of year. Scarlet anemones and rosy-lilac gazelles' horns, or yellow aspalathus. We search for various types of small lilies, with rippling, rose-like sheen, our tense gazes like closed petals, bursting towards their ripeness, as if we are redrawing the freedom of release from the closed borders imposed upon us.

We complete our tour, and the small bird with the closed eye is wrapped in the shawl against my chest, and we took him along with us.

At home, I named him Robin, based on the assurances of our bird-loving neighbour. When I expressed my doubt about the name due to the incomplete red ruff on his neck feathers, he told me: 'This is a young bird. The full red has not yet appeared on his feathers.'

At home, I put him under a sieve made of metal wire and left him some water and seeds. The first day passed and he was rigid and motionless. He stood frozen, as if he had been glued in place. He could not be seen clearly between the thin metal wires, as his dark colouring blended with the metal. He was unmoving and did not budge. I recalled the day a canary froze in my house, when his cage accidentally fell from the window ledge while I was out. The shock had caused it to stand frozen in place for two days without eating or drinking. Thus, I assessed that Robin would get better after a day or two.

It seemed to me then that however small birds are they have expressions and we can understand how they feel from their appearance. Movement is a sign of happiness. I put down some seeds and water for him and at night I felt pleased because he was in a safe place. He did not move the next day either, but a few seeds were missing from the handful that I had put in the dish.

I had to wait, listening to the Israeli loudspeakers circulating with the Jeeps for three more days until they announced the lifting of the curfew. During that time Robin did not move and he did not make a sound. There was nothing to indicate that he was getting better except his closed eye, which began to open little by little, although it remained smaller than his main, healthy eye.

I asked our neighbour, the bird breeder, whether I should keep him or release him. He assured me that Robin was a wild bird and could not endure captivity if he lived in a cage inside the house and that the best thing was definitely to return him to the wild as soon as possible before he became depressed and stopped eating and drinking.

I tossed and turned for a long time in bed, lying, as I did every night, in an impromptu position, in fear of the thundering clashes during the night. I battled unsuccessfully that premature, early-morning wakefulness that embitters my day, like the punishment of prisons. For no matter how securely the windows are closed, the reverberation of the loudspeakers penetrates the walls bringing us the voice of the Israeli officer, who in his poor, grammatically incorrect Arabic, filled with linguistic errors, orders us to stay in our houses that day, or informs us of the required time we must return home in the event that the curfew is lifted for a few hours.

It was an unpleasant morning, its disquiet relieved only by my preparations for the pleasing idea of returning Robin to his original habitat, to that spot where we had walked on that radiant day.

I did not have enough time because the curfew would soon be lifted and I had to return him to his original place, then go to stand in the long queue at the bakery, and afterwards scour the few shops for some vegetables.

My friend and I went by car to the western side of the city. In my hands was the metal sieve, which covered the dish in which Robin stood. The place was not beautiful, as we had thought it last time. There was a housing development occupying its edges turning it into a pit with newly built flats multiplying in it, lined up in haphazard, random rows, with scrap metal, piles of earth and building materials in front of them.

We looked for a tree near where we had found him but were unsuccessful. We found only a small pine tree that had been accidentally left behind, far from the excavations of the building sites.

We walked over the small rocks, and the snatching thorns, and homes of wild brambles, their thorns tugging at our clothes, until we reached that tree, standing at almost the highest point among the hills.

The tree did not look like a safe refuge but there was no alternative except the low thorns entwined around the rocks. Robin would surely know how to handle himself because a few days in the house would not be enough to eliminate his wild instinct. I approached the tree and placed him on one of its short branches. To my great surprise, he fell to the ground and did not hold onto the branch. I rushed to him, picked him up, and placed him on another branch of the tree. It seemed as if there was some impediment to his attachment to the place, because he was falling off the tree immediately. Perhaps he was still suffering from dizziness and loss of balance!

Nevertheless, there was no alternative. So I ran after him when he flew at a low altitude, immediately afterwards falling near a smooth rock, and I picked him up again so as to put him back on the tree branch. He restrained himself a little this time but it was not long before he lost his balance and fell once more.

There was no possibility of giving up, and time was running out. I had to return with my friend before it became dangerously late. He showed a little improvement at keeping his balance, trying to fly again each time. I could not take him back with me, and he had to hurry up and fly before he was finished off by the cats in the neighbouring residential district.

The seventh time he flew several metres horizontally then fell.

And the eighth ... and after more than ten attempts, he flew.

He flew.

Not high enough, but enough to take him away from that place and towards another.

He flew! And he disappeared!

And I have not seen him again since that moment.

Not long after his departure, at the end of that spring, I was again walking in that area when I noticed something that I had always seen before but that had not entered my field of vision. One of the birds of prey was circling high above like a helicopter. Staring, searching for prey, that might be a small bird like Robin. After that I began to realise that that bird was spending his days constantly circling there above the high mountain, directly above that small tree.

A high mountain, under a blue sky looking down on hills and ancient olive trees, and mountains overlooking a captivating sea, invaded by colonising settlements advancing from the histories of ancient wars. Vines still encircle the ruins of the farmers' stone huts of long ago, and beside the sea nestle cities, whose inhabitants have left and others have taken over, after wars that have continued for decades.

All that under one sky!

Is that why Robin flew far away and I have not seen him again since that moment?

Translated by Becki Maddock

RABA'I AL-MADHOUN

Excerpt from The Lady from Tel Aviv

My seatmate goes on talking as if we come from the same country. As if we share the same fears, the same constellations of film stars. As she recounts stories about the festival, my mind recalls televised scenes of the war – the live coverage of American attacks that sowed democracy across Iraq. The tonnes of ordnance that went into ploughing deep furrows across the burning old fields of despotism.

I let her talk and wander off in my mind to Asqalan, where her boyfriend plays basketball. Majdal Asqalan is where the protagonist of my novel is from. His whole family is from there. If he, Adel El-Bashity, could hear what she is saying, he would shout: 'If only our conflict took place in stadiums! If only the shots fired were at goals, not on people, we would have already founded a Democratic State of Football that stretched from the Mediterranean to the Jordan River, and there would be enough room for all footballers to live there in peace and harmony!' Sometimes Adel's optimism seems ridiculous to me, and it makes me chuckle to imagine that even football could peacefully coexist between the two sides in the foreseeable future. It would be more like El Salvador and Honduras in the 1969 World Cup qualifiers – when football led to war.

She stops talking, and I don't want to interrupt the silence. But she turns to me though realising only now that she has gone on too long or shared too much. Coyly, she asks, 'I'm sorry – where did you say you were from?'

The question surprises me. From the moment I sat down in my seat until the moment she asks the question, it has been bothering me. At first I am nervous, too unsettled to choose an answer. I could say, for instance, that I am Greek or Cypriot or Lebanese, or anything. I could pick any other nationality – anything but Palestinian. I am afraid someone might overhear and shout out: 'Palestinian! This man's a Palestinian!' What if someone got up and made a public announcement, 'Ladies and gentlemen: please be advised that there is a Palestinian on board!'

If this had been my seatmate's first question, I might not have answered it. But now, after getting to know each other, I am not in a position to ignore her. Whatever apprehensions I may have, they belong to the past. Still, I decide to play dumb. 'Where am I from? You never asked. You never asked.'

'No, I've asked you twice now.' And then wryly, she repeats it again.

'I am Palestinian. I have British citizenship, but I am Palestinian.'

'Aha. A Palestinian, huh?' she says. It is as if I had tried to put one over on her, or my answer is not good enough. She plays with a strand of her hair. Under the faint overhead light, it has lost most of its golden sheen.

Flatly, even coldly now, she asks, 'Are you taking a tour of Israel?'

'No, I am visiting family in Gaza.'

'Gaza?' She actually gasps as she says it.

'Yes. Gaza.'

She stops playing with her hair and turns toward the window to hide her reaction. She rests her chin on her hand and stares out. The window has now turned into a small black mirror that casts shadows over things we may think but cannot see. All around us the jet engines hum in a din so constant it sounds like nothing.

My seatmate turns away from her mirror and asks in a trembling voice: 'Do you often visit Gaza?'

'Not at all. This will be my first trip in thirty-eight years. The truth is that I haven't seen my mother in that long.'

She blots upright in her seat. 'My God! Thirty-eight years! How have you managed to stay away from your mother and family all these years? You're not a negligent son, are you? You don't look cruel, but ... I'm sorry for your mother.'

'The occupation is what's cruel. Not me ...'

She does not comment. I begin to rattle on as my bitterness gets the better of me, 'I haven't been able to go back since 1967. I was not allowed to go back.'

'Of course, of course. I hadn't thought of that. I am really sorry. It hadn't occurred to me that you were unable to visit ... Gaza, huh?'

'Yes. I'm going there with my new British passport. I just got it. Without it, I couldn't go via Tel Aviv.'

For some unknown reason, I begin to tell her my life story. She listens with interest and curiosity. She watches me without interrupting or saying a word, her head propped in the gap between our seats. She studies me as if I were spinning a fantastic yarn.

'I was born in 1948, in Asdud. In the place you now call Ashdod. My family left during the war, went to Gaza, along with so many others from southern Palestine. We fled there and settled. I spent my childhood and youth in the camps of Khan Yunis. I was educated in Gaza all through secondary school. When I finished, I went to study at Cairo University. After graduating, I wandered the world, a refugee standing on his own two feet – though one was made of exodus without end, and the other a journey without destination. I collected my exiles one by one, I labelled them according to the numbers of years I lived in each. I watch history in our part of the world and notice that it weighs our existence on a broken scale. For every Jewish immigrant to Israel, a dozen Palestinians are driven out.' Then I add: 'If it seems lopsided, it's because the scale that measures us has never been balanced.'

My seatmate takes refuge in silence. She does not put up any resistance to my last attack, which, in any case, was not one I had planned to make. Instead, she sends whatever anxiety she is feeling out into the night sky. She studies herself in the blank mirror. At the same time, her hand creeps over and gently clasps mine.

Returning from her distant musings, she twists to face me. Her fingers send warmth across my hand. 'I hope you have no delays in seeing your mother and that you have a good time together. I hope that there can be peace between us and the Palestinians. We're tired of the situation, all of us. The problem is not the people, it's the politicians. Our politicians and yours. Sharon doesn't want peace, nor does Arafat.' As she speaks, she retracts her hand and shifts her weight onto the forearm that rests between our seats.

The extremists on your side and the extremists on ours. They always say that when they want to parse the crime and reapportion blame for the shedding of Palestinian blood. Your extremists and our extremists. Fine. I'd love to answer her with a simple quote from Mahmoud Darwish: get out. Leave our lands. Evacuate our territories and quit our sea. Get out of our wheat, our salt, our wounds. Leave the vocabulary of our memory. Then – and only then – can you take care of your extremists while we take care of ours.

I say none of this to her. What is the use of dredging up the entire Middle Eastern conflict in a fleeting meeting between two strangers sitting next to each on a flight? When I do talk, I say something else entirely: I tell her that I hope Palestinians and Israelis might leave the battlefield behind them and learn to share a life together. I hope that one day she and I might walk together a long a long road with no checkpoints between us.

No assassinations and no suicide bombers, no soldiers and no militants, no Zionism and no Palestinian national liberation, no Intifadas and no settlements, no Sharons and no Arafats, no Abu Mazens and no Shaul Mofazes, no warlords, no settlers, no Apache helicopters, no F-16s and no car bombs. I hope that we could be just two regular passengers passing the night on any flight ...

Translated by Elliott Colla

SELMA DABBAGH

Excerpt from Out of It

It did not take long for the newspaper to upset him. He had read the Sheikh A bin B meets Sheikh B bin A to discuss bilateral relations bit, skimmed the runaway housemaids and discontented manual labourers section, sought and found some hidden nuggets of adultery charges and rogue sexual activity and (oh joy!) he even found a piece about further evidence of lesbian activity in school bathrooms. Jibril chuckled happily. Un-Islamic behaviour tickled him to the core.

He braced himself as he turned over the page to the International Section, his eye automatically finding the news from home. The same images seemed to have been repeating themselves for years now, the perpetual cycle of violence and diplomatic grins, dead child – stone-throwing youths – exploded car – crying woman outside a demolished house – grinning leadership – dead child again. 'The worse the loss, the more we grin,' Jibril said, staring at a particularly despicable picture of the leaders standing on a golf course in Texas.

'They treat their dogs better than us,' said the young man behind the counter, gazing at the sprightly labrador at the President's feet, 'A dog's life would be a blessing compared to what some of us have to live through,' he nodded, this time to the picture of a mother crying over her dead child.

'Where are you from?' Jibril had been having problems reconciling the boy's face and Arabic with his badge, 'Hi!' it said, 'I am

ERNESTO. Welcome to Starbright®. I am happy to serve you.' If he had to guess, he would have said the boy was the same as he was, only brought up in Jordan, 'Mr Ernesto?'

'Oh no, that's only my work name,' the boy said turning to Jibril from the milk steamer that was hawking and spitting behind him, 'HQ designates our names and market research has found that Spanish names are more amenable to the clientele. My true name is Abu Wazir, Salem Abu Wazir.'

'Abu Wazir? You are from? You are from my village?' Jibril named his village, to which the manager raised his eyebrows.

'You know the Abu Wazirs? You know my family?' The café was filling out. A woman with prawn skin was leaning down close to Jibril's legs tapping over a chocolate cake with a fingernail, her cleavage a gathering of creases and sunspots.

'Know your family? *Know* your family?' Jibril exclaimed, 'I practically am your family! I am Jibril Mujahed, the Mujaheds and the Abu Wazirs have married each other for years. Centuries in fact, since the time of the crusades.' The boy laid out a piece of cake on a plate for his customer and looked up, bemused.

'I've heard of you, uncle. You were with the Outside Leadership, were you not?' The boy was a bit spotty. His pimples had white tips and clustered together around his nostrils. Other than that, he would be a fairly good-looking chap if he calmed down on the hair cream a bit.

'I was with the Organisation. Yes. Not anymore though. Left it years ago. And you're? A manager here?'

'I manage all the airport branches. We had two outlets when I started, now we have fourteen. It's a growth industry.'

'A franchise, I suppose?'

'Of course;' the boy, Salem Abu Wazir (Abu Wazir, eh?) turned back to his staff. A queue was forming of servicemen, businessmen and backpackers. All pushed up behind Jibril to see into the counter. Jibril thought of trying to recreate their village using the salt and pepper pots to show this boy where the Abu Wazir house had been compared to the Mujahed's, but it would be difficult as the village had been built on the slopes of two hills and the houses had been like cubes stacked up the sides.

Jibril could quite clearly see and feel himself as a child in Palestine. When he was there he wore shorts and a dangly belt, always (the outfit had been frozen in a photograph). Behind him, the village was a series of blocks and arches, rough stone straddling from one building to another in semi-circles, arched windows, domes smoothed over with sand and outdoor staircases. There were days where the smell of his village would come and sit on his nose like a flirtatious djinn. He would wake from a dream and feel himself boyish, a spirit running through alleyways, over roofs, in the olive groves, leaping in the sun, a sun that was always bright but never harsh. And then at other times (it was there in him), when he had maybe drunk a bit too much, or been talking to someone who knew his village, or a similar village, he would suddenly feel like saying, 'Yes, that place! How about it? How about we go back and see how that place is doing?' as though he had just gone around a corner and if he were to turn back quickly enough it would be there. But it would take less time than the words took to get to his mouth for him to realise that it was absurd. He could never go back to that place, it had been sealed off to him forever, blown to the sky with explosives then flattened to the ground with bulldozers, built over with tarmac, lived on top of by other people. People of a faith he didn't have.

He tried to go back to his newspaper, but Abu Wazir, eh? This boy an Abu Wazir? He wished it would stop affecting him. He wished he didn't care. He wished that he were free of it all. It was now almost eight years since he left the Organisation and all political involvement with it, but it still got to him. When Jibril announced that he was leaving, their Leader had looked him hard in the eye, 'You can leave the Organisation, Jibril,' he had said, 'Of course, Jibril, we do not want you to leave, for you to leave is your choice. But Jibril you must understand that you can leave the Organisation but the Organisation will never leave you.' Jibril still did not know what that meant, but to be safe he had decided to treat it as a threat.

It was true though, people still acted as though he was part of it, 'This is Jibril Mujahed of the Palestine Liberation Organisation' his Western friends would say, as though they had a piranha in their fish tank, and he had no idea how they knew. The Arabs would just mouth 'the Organisation,' at each other; 'Jibril was with the Organisation,' they would say with a nod and that was enough.

Enough for some of them, particularly those who had been in Kuwait, to never stop banging on about the fraction of their salary that had been deducted every month to support the cause. 'So your children went to school in Switzerland, did they? And us? Kicked us out of our homes in Kuwait because of your leadership and then what? Left to rot, the education of our children disrupted, and you? Educated your children in Switzerland, did you? So where's our five percent? Lost it in the casinos of Monaco, did you? While our families rot in the refugee camps? Bravo my friend, bravo!' He never encouraged any of this talk about the Organisation. No, he never encouraged such discussions. There was nothing he could do anyway. It was all in the past.

Not for the first time Jibril offered up a prayer of gratitude to this Gulf State that had taken him in despite his background and his papers, or lack thereof, and had allowed him to work. He thanked the glittering forest of Duty Free shops around him, complete with their electronic moose heads singing Christmas carols, the three-floor high columns of mirrors, the polished four-wheel drives displayed high on velvet platforms. He even thanked the posterior of the cleaner squeezing out her mop. I'm so glad to be here. I'm so glad to be out of it. He had done his bit. No one could hold him to account for the Organisation's mistakes. No one. He had wiped his hands of it long ago.

'I'm waiting for my daughter,' Jibril announced when it quietened down, 'She's coming from Gaza.'

'I didn't know that was possible,' the Abu Wazir boy said.

'Not directly of course. She's gone through the borders into Egypt and then been flown out. They held her up for days.' In the middle distance an electronic tape of red dots was revolving around a screen informing Jibril and other potential customers about the discounts in the electronics store, particularly the substantial reductions on portable DVDs.

'You're sure that she got on the plane?'

'Yes, yes. She got on, and she's here. They're just asking her a few questions. Nothing to worry about.' Nothing that he knew he should be worried about, but of course it was possible that they had picked up on something. The message he had heard was that she, his mousy little daughter, his Iman, named after the belly-dancing star of all stars of the Cairo nights, was trying to get herself mixed up with some Islamic movement. Well, she would be backing the right horse there, if she wanted to side with the winning team. That lot were popping up everywhere: elections, coups, terrorist stunts. All action, that lot. Could not stand them himself, so dour and sanctimonious. He had never had any time for religion and saw no reason to change: God had hardly smiled on them this far; in fact he had verily shat upon them.

Silly girl. He would give her a good talking to. That was all it would need.

More red dots. This time the text stopped and flashed before him several times before rolling along. Even the main Japanese brands had come down in price. Sixty percent off the original price for DVDs. Flash. Flash. Sixty percent!

'Terrible,' said the boy, 'How old is she?'

'Twenty-five,' Jibril replied although he had the feeling he had been saying that for a couple of years now.

'Terrible,' said the man again, 'It appears that it is our destiny to get hassled in these places; airports, borders, checkpoints. That's our unifying national destiny.'

'Yes,' Jibril agreed, 'Yes, yes,' His tongue was dried out from the coffee. 'Yes,' Jibril said, shaking hands. He considered buying Iman a present: a shawl, some jewellery, a peaked cap with a designer name on it, a diamante pin, a stuffed camel, a box of dates. She would need so many things that he was not really sure where to start. He squeezed, rubbed and stroked many potential gifts and found out their prices, colours and sizes and had reached the cash till with armfuls of goods when he decided it best to leave it for Suzi to get things for his daughter. She could take Iman to the malls. Lots of time for sorting her out.

Happy with the thought of Suzi's adoption of Iman's upbringing (and feminisation; the girl really should be thinking of settling down), Jibril sauntered into the electronics section, where he remained, haggling over several seven- to eight-inch screens, until the fixer called to say that they were both through.

RAMZY BAROUD

Excerpt from The Last Earth: A Palestinian Story

Under the Open Sky: How Beit Daras Was Lost

When the war was about to start, Ahmad al-Haaj was in his second year at his Gaza high school. Much of the fighting was taking place in other parts of Palestine, mostly near areas where Jewish settlements and towns held military sway over largely disorganised local fighters.

When Arab fighters attempted to cut off the few Jewish settlements in the south from the rest of the Zionist command, several fighters were killed and their actions instead resulted in the blockading of the main Arab roads. This meant that Ahmad, along with seven other students, could not return to their villages north of Gaza, a predicament that compelled the school's headmaster to appeal to a responsive British officer who managed to sneak the frightened students in the back of a congested supplies truck back to Al-Majdal, but not further than that.

Dropped in Al-Majdal, they still had to walk five, eight, twelve, and in the case of one student, fifteen miles through dangerous terrain to reach their villages.

When Ahmad arrived in Al-Sawafir on 8 April 1948, he learned that Arab fighters under the command of Abdul Qader al-Husseini lost Qastal, west of Al-Quds, and that the Zionists attacked the village of Deir Yassin and slaughtered almost half of its inhabitants. All the roads that led to Al-Sawafir were subsequently closed; the one between Al-Sawafir and Masmiyeh, the one near Qastina, the one close to Be'er Toviya, the road between Masmiyeh and Al-Quds, near Khalda; even Al-Quds itself was nearly isolated now that Deir Yassin was conquered.

Word of mouth brought news of similar massacres in the following days. The neighbourhoods in Al-Quds were falling one after the other, starting with Sheikh Jarrah. Yafa itself fell later in April, followed by Haifa. Many of the terrified residents managed to flee as they were chased out with nothing but the clothes on their backs. But many were killed or fell prey to execution by gunfire or grenades. And not all of those who rushed to the open sea were lucky enough to jump into stable vessels or the fishing boats that remained afloat. Entire families watched each other drown, their screams swallowed up by an unforgiving mother nature.

To buy his German rifle and 125 bullets, Ahmad's father, Khaleel al-Haaj sold a cow and four dunums. Laughter roared across his village as some found his action hasty and excessive. The Arab League had promised to send its armies to liberate Palestine, but it did not take a young communist like Ahmad long to realise that the rag-tag Arab armies, mostly operating under the command of the same colonial powers that handed Palestine to the Zionists in the first place, were not capable of fighting a liberation war. Only when the Arabs did not arrive did the fellahin understand the depth of their crisis, prompting some to follow suit and obtain rifles in a crazed rush.

Just as the large Palestinian cities were about to fall to the militias, Arab paramilitaries were sent to aid Palestinian fighters, as a first step before the anticipated arrival of the official armies. But with time, it was becoming clearer that the Arabs were belatedly joining the war with the understanding that they were not to venture into areas designated for the proposed Jewish state.

Egyptian units arrived through Sinai, reached the Gaza district, and moved towards Iraq Suwaydan, hoping to reach Bir al-Sabi, and as far as al-Khalil, Beit Jibrin, and Bethlehem.

As for the Arab Salvation Army, led by a French-trained Lebanese officer, Fawzi al-Qawuqji, it entered Palestine through the Galilee, ostensibly to reach Yafa, Haifa, and Nazareth. The latter paramilitary units were quickly routed and regrouped back in the Galilee once the main cities fell and their inhabitants were killed, expelled, or fled.

Al-Sawafir itself had ten fighters, one of whom was Khaleel al-Haaj. While Arab militaries were losing the war, the fellahin were winning small battles in the south. Fighters with old Turkish rifles would gather from the nearby villages and move towards whichever village was likely to be attacked. In the second battle of Beit Daras, when the Jewish settlement of Be'er Tuvia mounted another failed attack, the villagers held their positions yet again, still hoping that the Egyptian army would arrive soon and defeat Be'er Tuvia once and for all.

Ahmad was shaken by the sight of the dead bodies collected by the Red Cross as Arab fighters were celebrating their victory. But he did not dare show any sign of weakness and held back the emotions engulfing his fledgling manhood. His father Khaleel also took part in that battle where he used twenty bullets, and, by the end of the fight, had nine to spare. Beit Daras, whose inhabitants were known for their oddly large heads, generosity and impatience, had twelve rifles and a total of 967 bullets, all equally distributed among the toughest men in the village.

When the triumphant Al-Sawafir fighters returned proudly to their village from Beit Daras, holding up their rifles and chanting their cheers, the immensity of the victory was overshadowed by the understanding that the Zionist militants were likely to return with bigger guns and more fighters.

The fellahin fighters had no time to lose to formulate a strategy, and met in Ahmad al-Haaj's new house, the one built with bricks and a tiled roof. Their humble leadership was composed of three mukhtars and elderly men representing the most esteemed families. They were all men who had never imagined they would be drawing up war plans. Using nothing but their intuition as their guide, their decision was for the fighters to secure the main road, and others to join in using knives and clubs once a call for help was issued through the chants of 'Allahu Akbar' should the village be attacked. And it was attacked. Zionist militants moved in large numbers, all travelling in fortified military vehicles. Some of these were gifted or abandoned by the British and others purchased for the purpose of this war. Each military convoy consisted of anywhere between forty to fifty cars, with operations based on a set of military strategies that was aimed at isolating large areas before moving in to empty a besieged village of its inhabitants, exacting whatever price was required in blood and destruction.

In many cases, once the population of a village was banished, the remaining residents who did not leave due to pride, ill-health or an elderly body were pitilessly murdered and the village then looted and burned to the ground. Yet despite their defeat in Beit Daras, the militias seemed to direct their focus elsewhere, far away from Al-Sawafir and its ten fighters. That was the case until the Egyptian army officially entered the war on 15 April 1948, the same day the British formally left their positions, thus relinquishing Palestine and leaving the Zionist militias in control of most major cities.

But even then, Ahmad skilfully moved about between the villages, guardedly but with relative ease, using dirt side roads and avoiding the main road where the ten fighters and his father hid warily in the bushes, dreading the return of military convoys. Miraculously, Ahmad even went to Al-Majdal to sell harvested and milled wheat to purchase bullets for his father's German rifle.

A feeling of hope and relative stability began to return when the Egyptians deployed some army units from Sinai, through Rafah, to Gaza City, which they designated as their headquarters and then moved north. Upon their arrival in Gaza, they were joined by many volunteers, including Ahmad Ismail, the physics teacher at Imam al-Shafi'i High School.

The first full-scale battle fought by the Egyptian army was a success. On 17 May they surrounded Yad Mordechai kibbutz, a few miles to the south of Asqalan, for four days and finally conquered the fortified settlement with the help of local Gaza fighters who were later assigned fixed salaries from the Egyptian army for their bravery. On 19 May they reached the town of Al-Majdal, where they met with various volunteer forces who also enlisted in the Egyptian army. These volunteers, under the command of Mostafa Hafez, were the core of what was later known as fedayeen, Palestine's freedom fighters.

The Egyptians continued their drive further north to Iraq Suwaydan, then curved slightly to the east to Al-Faluja on their way to Bayt Jibrin in the direction of Al-Khalil. Their intention was to remain within the borders of the proposed Arab state, and not to go beyond the boundaries of the coastal area of that state somewhere between Rafah and Isdud.

The state set aside for the Palestinian Arabs per the United Nations partition plan of the previous year, was less than half of the original size of Palestine, even though the Arabs then constituted the vast majority of the country's population.

The Zionist militia convoys eventually returned, with a vengeance. They made their expected move against Beit Daras on 5 June. Striking at dawn, they charged against the village until the early afternoon hours. By placating the stubborn Beit Daras, they knew the entire structure of local resistance was likely to fragment and collapse, so they proceeded to surround the village from all directions. All roads leading to it were cut off to ensure that fellahin fighters could not come to the rescue.

By then the fighters in Beit Daras had acquired up to ninety rifles, but the invading militias had amassed an arsenal of modern weapons including mortars, machine-guns mounted on top of fortified vehicles and hundreds of fully armed troops. The fellahin did not stand a chance.

Within the first hour of fighting, Beit Daras was on fire. Those who could not fight attempted to quell the flames of treason, but to no avail. Those who managed to escape ran to the Egyptian army, stationed only three miles north. But their frenzied calls for help and the destruction they described was not enough to implore these comrades to help them. The commander told the beseeching locals they could not intervene as they had not been given the orders to do so. Worse still, they even refused to supply the villagers with weapons or ammunition to defend themselves, for that also required a signature from the general command in Gaza.

It was too late anyway. By then the militias had moved in, and executed survivors of the initial onslaught, civilians and all, whoever they were – men, women, children – it made no difference. There were neither rules of war nor rules of engagement. Some escaped running through burning fields, tripping on one another while chased by sniper bullets. The few who remained alive arrived in Joura, Al-Majdal, Hamameh and the other nearby villages. The demise of Beit Daras had crushed the spirit of the smaller and less defendable villages.

The massacre instilled fear and horror, especially as the death toll reached three hundred in a village with a population that barely totalled two thousand.

The mukhtars of the much smaller Al-Sawafir met again and resolved that Be'er Toviya was likely to continue its attacks now that the heart of resistance went up in flames. They urged the people to sleep in open fields so that their homes were not burned in the middle of the night while they were still inside. Terrified and unsure of the plan that guaranteed nothing, hundreds of families walked late at night to nowhere in particular, hauling whatever food they could salvage, and pushing along their cattle and donkeys. They all slept under the open sky, with the intention of returning in the morning to salvage whatever else they could carry – their chickens, the remaining flour, bottles of olive oil, small stacks of corn and lentils.

FADY JOUDAH

Mimesis

My daughter
wouldn't hurt a spider
That had nested
Between her bicycle handles
For two weeks
She waited
Until it left of its own accord

If you tear down the web I said
It will simply know
This isn't a place to call home
And you'd get to go biking

She said that's how others
Become refugees isn't it?

Immune

My heart isn't another's
love is no transplant

it can be
or when I'm dead

I will give you my eyes & also my liver
you must suppress their memory of me

Sleeping Trees

Between what should and what should not be
Everything is liable to explode. Many times
I was told who has no land has no sea. My father
Learned to fly in a dream. This is the story
Of a sycamore tree he used to climb
When he was young to watch the rain.

Sometimes it rained so hard it hurt. Like being
Beaten with sticks. Then the mud would run red.

My brother believed bad dreams could kill
A man in his sleep, he insisted
We wake my father from his muffled screams
On the night of the day he took us to see his village.
No longer his village he found his tree amputated.
Between one falling and the next

There's a weightless state. There was a woman
Who loved me. Asked me how to say tree
In Arabic. I didn't tell her. She was sad. I didn't understand.
When she left, I saw a man in my sleep three times. A man I knew
Could turn anyone into one-half reptile.
I was immune. I thought I was. I was terrified of being

The only one left. When we woke my father
He was running away from soldiers. Now
He doesn't remember that night. He laughs
About another sleep, he raised his arms to strike a king
And tried not to stop. He flew
But mother woke him and held him for an hour,

Or half an hour, or as long as it takes a migration inward.
Maybe if I had just said it,
Shejerah, she would've remembered me longer. Maybe
I don't know much about dreams
But my mother taught me the law of omen. The dead
Know about the dying and sometimes
Catch them in sleep like the sycamore tree
My father used to climb

When he was young to watch the rain stream,
And he would gently swing.

Still Life

You write your name on unstained glass
So you're either broken or seen through

When it came time for the affidavit
The panel asked how much art
Over the blood of strangers the word

Mentioned the weather and the sleepers
Under the weather all this
Was preceded by tension enzymatic
To the hills behind us and the forests ahead

Where children don't sleep
In resting tremor and shelling
The earth is a pomegranate

A helmet ochre or copper sinks
In buoyant salt water
Divers seek its womb despite its dura mater
And it hangs on trees like pregnant mistletoes

I'll stand next to one
And have my German lover

Remember me on a Mediterranean island
Though she would eventually wed
An Israeli once she'd realised
What she wanted from life

A mother of two

On the nose of Mount Carmel
Where my wife's father was born driven out

My father's hands depearl
The fruit in a few minutes add a drop
Of rose water some shredded coconut
For us to gather around him

He will lead his grandchildren out transfer
Bundles of pine branches in the yard to where
His tomatoes and cucumbers grow in summer

Let them let them
Gather the dried pine needles forever he says
They will refuse to believe the fire dies

And they will listen to his first fire
On a cold night in a forest of eucalyptus trees
The British had planted as natural reserve
Outside Gaza

HANAN ASHRAWI

Hadeel's Song

Some words are hard to pronounce –
He-li-cop-ter is most vexing
(A-pa-che or Co-bra is impossible)
But how it can stand still in the sky
I cannot understand –
What holds it up
What bears its weight
(Not clouds, I know)
It sends a flashing light – so smooth –
It makes a deafening sound
The house shakes
(There are holes in the wall by my bed)
Flash-boom-light-sound –
And I have a hard time sleeping
(I felt ashamed when I wet my bed, but no one scolded me).

Plane – a word much easier to say –
It flies, tayyara,
My mother told me
A word must have a meaning
A name must have a meaning
Like mine,
(Hadeel, the cooing of the dove)
Tanks, though, make a different sound

They shudder when they shoot
Dabbabeh is a heavy word
As heavy as its meaning.

Hadeel – the dove – she coos
Tayyara – she flies
Dabbabeh – she crawls
My Mother – she cries
And cries and cries
My Brother – Rami – he lies
DEAD
And lies and lies, his eyes
Closed.
Hit by a bullet in the head
(bullet is a female lead – rasasa – she kills,
my pencil is a male lead – rasas – he writes)
What's the difference between a shell and a bullet?
(What's five-hundred-milli-metre-
Or eight-hundred-milli-metre-shell?)
Numbers are more vexing than words –
I count to ten, then ten-and-one, ten-and-two
But what happens after ten-and-ten,
How should I know?
Rami, my brother, was one
Of hundreds killed –
They say thousands are hurt,
But which is more
A hundred or a thousand (miyyeh or alf)
I cannot tell –
So big – so large – so huge –
Too many, too much.

Palestine – Falasteen – I'm used to,
It's not so hard to say,
It means we're here – to stay –
Even though the place is hard
On kids and mothers too
For soldiers shoot
And airplanes shell
And tanks boom
And tear gas makes you cry
(Though I don't think it's tear gas that makes my mother cry)
I'd better go and hug her
Sit in her lap a while
Touch her face (my fingers wet)
Look in her eyes
Until I see myself again
A girl within her mother's sight.

If words have meaning, Mama,
What is Is-ra-el?
What does a word mean
if it is mixed
with another –
If all soldiers, tanks, planes and guns are
Is-ra-el-i
What are they doing here
In a place I know
In a word I know – (Palestine)
In a life that I no longer know?

From the Diary of an Almost-Four-Year-Old

Tomorrow, the bandages
will come off. I wonder
will I see half an orange,
half an apple, half my
mother's face
with my one remaining eye?
I did not see the bullet
but felt its pain
exploding in my head.
His image did not
vanish, the soldier
with a big gun, unsteady
hands, and a look in
his eyes
I could not understand.

If I can see him so clearly
with my eyes closed,
it could be that inside our heads
we each have one spare set
of eyes
to make up for the ones we lose.

Next month, on my birthday,
I'll have a brand-new glass eye,
maybe things will look round
and fat in the middle –
I've gazed through all my marbles,
they made the world look strange.

I hear a nine-month-old
has also lost an eye,
I wonder if my soldier
shot her too – a soldier
looking for little girls who
look him in the eye –
I'm old enough, almost four,
I've seen enough of life,
but she's just a baby
who didn't know any better.

SAYED KASHUA

On Nakba Day

On Nakba Day I can't stop thinking about my grandmother. If only she were still alive; if only she was the way I like to remember her: strong, sharp-witted, always waiting for me after another day of school, sitting on her lambs' wool prayer rug. I would shrug off my heavy book bag and run to her, bury my head in her bosom and silently weep.

'Why are you crying again, my child?' She could sense my body trembling.

'They keep picking on me,' I would tell her. 'They keep picking on me and won't let me breathe.'

'Who?' she would ask. 'Tell me who and I'll show them what's what.'

'Everybody,' I'd answer her. 'And my friends are worse than the others.'

'That's how it is.' I'd like to hear her say that now, just like then, as she stroked my head. 'Because you're a smart boy, the smartest, and they all want to be like you but they can't.'

If I'm so smart, Grandma, then how do you explain the fact that I still haven't figured out how to get along in life? If I'm so smart, how do you explain the terrible fears? And, yes, I'm sorry: I no longer sleep with a small Koran under my pillow, as you taught me to do when I was young. I want to tell you that it never helped, Grandma, I was always afraid at night, and now more than ever. Except I no longer have anywhere to escape to, there's nowhere to hide. And you know, I'm a father now and I have children who get scared at night and come to me to hide. Three children, Grandma. Sometimes I tell them the same bedtime stories you used to tell me.

I told them how you used to have these huge watermelons that you would load on the backs of a convoy of camels, to take to the sea to be loaded on boats. I told them about the cows, the donkeys and the horses. About how on holidays you would dress up in a man's clothes, put on an abaya and a keffiyeh, and gallop on the horse together with Grandpa all the way to Jaffa. About the café in Jaffa and how you always told us about the city women who sat there shamelessly smoking narghiles just like the men.

'But so did you!' I would always say, laughing, and you would answer: 'Yes, but no one knew I was a woman, not like those wanton Jaffa women. You should have seen them, coming into the theatre after us and sitting next to us, those loose women, may God roast them in the fires of hell.'

But the other stories, Grandma, the ones that made you emotional, that made you cry when you told them, those I haven't yet dared to tell. Sometimes I think I wouldn't want my kids to have to bear that burden, maybe because I want to give them the illusion that a home is a permanent thing, strong, protective, so they wouldn't fear, as I do, a disaster lurking just beyond the doorstep. So I haven't yet told them that Grandpa was killed in the '48 war and I haven't told them how you became a young widow. I haven't told them about your lands, which were all lost. Or about the bullets that whistled all around and the shells that fell right and left.

I haven't told them about how you hunched over your baby son, my father, in the wheat fields, using your own body to protect him from the fire, and how you always used to say at that point, 'as if my body would have really protected him if the fire would have caught me it would have taken him, too, but at least I would have died before my son.'

So I don't tell them that one, or the most terrible of all your stories, about that moment when the shelling ceased and silence suddenly descended, that moment when you tried to go and bring food from the field for your children and you saw that nothing was the same anymore. I remember that look, Grandma, that same look on your face each one of the thousands of times you described that awful day, always the same look, with eyes glazed over with tears in just the same way. And I remember you always pulling out your handkerchief with that same delicate motion, and saying, 'In that one moment I understood that everything I had was lost.'

How hard it is to live with this feeling, with the constant fear of the future, the idea that I must always be prepared for the worst. The feeling that at any moment everything I have could be lost. That a house is never a certainty and that refugee-hood is a sword hanging over me.

Meanwhile, I've become a storyteller myself. In a language you wouldn't understand, but don't worry: not that many people who speak it really understand. Sometimes I feel like I'm basically telling all the same stories I heard from you, and just like you used to do, I repeat them time after time in all different ways and all different forms, to no avail. People here aren't ready to believe your stories, Grandma, or mine. If only you were here now, on this Nakba Day, I would get on a horse and gallop all the way home, ask your forgiveness for having run away from you in your final days, and bury my head in your bosom for more silent weeping.

'Why are you crying, my child?'

If you only knew what I go through, if you only knew how hard it is to tell stories.

'Who's picking on you? Tell me and I'll show them what's what.'

'Everybody, Grandma, and what really makes it hurt is I thought they were my friends.'

'That's how it is,' I know you would have said, as you stroked my head until the trembling stopped. And then you'd say: 'So, are you hungry?'

LISA SUHAIR MAJAJ

Fifty Years On / Stones in an Unfinished Wall

1.

Fifty years on
I am trying to tell the story
of what was lost
before my birth

the story of what was there
before the stone house fell
mortar blasted loose
rocks carted away for new purposes, or smashed
the land declared clean, empty
before the oranges bowed in grief
blossoms sifting to the ground like snow
quickly melting
before my father clamped his teeth
    hard
          on the pit of exile
slammed shut the door to his eyes

before tears turned to disbelief
disbelief to anguish
anguish to helplessness
helplessness to rage
rage to despair

before the cup was filled
raised forcibly to our lips

fifty years on
I am trying to tell the story
of what we are still losing

2.
I am trying to find a home in history
but there is no more space in the books
for exiles

the arbiters of justice
have no time
for the dispossessed
without credentials

and what good are words
when there is no page
for the story?

3.
the aftersong filters down
like memory
echo of ash
history erased the names
of four hundred eighteen villages
emptied, razed

but cactus still rims the perimeters
emblem of what will not stay hidden
In the Jaffa district alone:

Al-'Abbasiyya
Abu Kishk
Bayt Dajan
Biyar 'Adas
Fajja
Al-Haram
Ijlil al-Qibliyya
Ijlil al-Shamaliyya
al-Jammasin al-Gharbi
al-Jammasin al-Sharqi
Jarisha
Kafr 'Ana
al-Khayriyya
al-Mas'udiyya
al-Mirr
al-Muwaylih
Ranitya
al-Safiriyya
Salama
Saqiya
al-Sawalima
al-Shaykh Muwannis
Yazur

all that remains
a scattering of stones and rubble
across a forgotten landscape

fifty years on
the words push through
a splintered song
forced out one note
at a time

4.
The immensity of loss
shrouds everything

in despair
we seek the particular

light angling gently
in single rays

the houses of Dayr Yasin
were built of stone, strongly built
with thick walls

a girls' school a boys' school a bakery
two guest-houses a social club a thrift fund
three shops four wells two mosques

a village of stone cutters
a village of teachers and shopkeepers

an ordinary village
with a peaceful reputation

until the massacre

carried out without discriminating
among men and women
children and old people

in the aftermath
light remembers

light searches out the hidden places
fills every crevice

light peers through windows
slides across neatly swept doorsteps
finds the hiding places of the children

light slips into every place
where the villagers were killed
the houses, the streets, the doorways
light traces the bloodstains

light glints off the trucks
that carried the men through the streets
like sheep before butchering

light pours into the wells
where they threw the bodies

light seeks out the places where sound
was silenced

light streams across stone
light stops at the quarry

5.
near Qisraya, circa 1938
a fisherman leans forward,
flings his net
across a sea slightly stirred
by wind

to his left
land tumbles
rocky blurred
to his right
sky is hemmed
by an unclear
horizon

(ten years
before the Nakbeh –

the future
already closing
down)

6.
fifty years later
shock still hollows the throats
of those driven out

without water, we stumbled into the hills

a small child lay beside the road
sucking the breast of its dead mother

outside Lydda
soldiers ordered everyone
to throw all valuables onto a blanket

one young man refused

almost casually,

the soldier pulled up his rifle
shot the man

he fell, bleeding and dying
his bride screamed and cried

he fell to the earth
they fell in despair to the earth

the earth held them
the earth soaked up their cries

their cries sank into the soil
filtered into underground streams

fifty springs on
their voices still rise from the earth

fierce as the poppies
that cry from the hills each spring

in remembrance

7.
some stories are told in passing
barely heard in the larger anguish

among those forced out
was a mother with two babies

one named Yasmine
and another

whose name no one remembers
her life so short
even its echo
is forgotten

the nameless child died on the march

it was a time of panic
no one could save a small girl

and so her face crumpled
lost beneath the weight of earth

I know only that she loved the moon
that lying ill on her mother's lap
she cried inconsolably
wanted to hold it in her hands
a child
she didn't know Palestine
would soon shine
    unreachable
as the moon

8.
the river floods its banks
littering the troubled landscape

we pick our way amid shards
heir to a generation
that broke their teeth on the bread of exile
that cracked their hearts on the stone of exile
necks bent beneath iron keys to absent doors

their lamentations
an unhealed wound

I was forced to leave my village
but the village refused to abandon me
my blood is there
my soul is flying in the sky over the old streets

fifty years on
soul still seeks a sky

9.
the walls were torn down long ago
homes demolished
rebuilding forbidden

but the stones remain

someone dug them from the soil
with bare hands
carried them across the fields

someone set the stones
in place on the terraced slope

someone planted trees,
dug wells

someone still waits in the fields all night
humming the old songs quietly

someone watches stars chip darkness

into dawn

someone remembers
how stone holds dew through the summer night

how stone
waits for the thirsty birds

ADANIA SHIBLI

Out of Time

My little watch is the first to sense the change going in to and out of Palestine. On the way there I notice it on my wrist, counting the time down to the second, waiting for the moment when the wheels of the plane touch the airport runway, and I set it to local time so it goes on counting it with an infinite familiarity. And as soon as I go out of Palestine it advances listlessly, taking its time parting with the local time there, which ends once the plane touches down in a foreign land.

It may seem to some I'm slightly exaggerating in what I'm telling about my watch, especially as it is a very little watch. People often are amazed how it can tell me the time at all, being so small. I myself could have yet shared their doubts had I not found out about watches and their secret powers.

It goes back to primary school, during one of the Arabic literature classes. The curriculum back then was, and it still is, subject to the approval of the Israeli Censorship Bureau, which embraced texts from various Arab countries, except for Palestine, fearing that these would contain references or even hints that could raise the pupils' awareness of the Palestinian question. Hence, Palestinian literature was considered unlawful, if not a taboo, similar to pornography – except for one text, 'Man and his Alarm Clock', a short story by Samira Azzam, which the Censorship Bureau found 'harmless'.

The story, published in 1963, tells of a young man preparing himself before he turns in, the night ahead of his very first day of work. He sets his alarm clock for four o'clock in the morning so as to catch the train in time to go to work. No sooner had the alarm clock gone off the next morning than there came a knocking at his front door. When he opens it, he finds before him an old man. He has no clue who this man is and he does not get the chance to ask him, as the latter turns and walks away, disappearing into the darkness. The same is repeated day after day so that the young man no longer sets his alarm clock. It is only after several months that he discovers who that old man is, after a colleague tells him this man goes knocking on the doors of all the employees in the company. He wakes them up on time in order for them not to be late for their train and meet their destiny as his own son did, who had one morning arrived late at the station, while the train was leaving. He held on to its door, but his hand betrayed him and he slipped down, falling underneath its wheels.

At first glance, the story may seem simple and 'safe', especially before the censor's eyes. Yet it actually contributed towards shaping my consciousness regarding the question of Palestine as no other text I have ever read in my life has done. Were there one day Palestinian employees who commuted to work by train? Was there a train station? Was there a train honking? Was there one day a normal life in Palestine? And where is it now and why has it gone?

The text, in turn, had engraved in my soul a deep sense of yearning for all that was – including the tragic – normal and banal, to a degree that I could no longer accept the marginalised, minor life to which we've been exiled since 1948, during which our existence turned into a 'problem'.

Against this story and the multiple modes of existence it revealed to me, stands my little watch. And my watch is more similar to that old man in Azzam's story than it is to a Swiss watch whose primary concern is to count time with precision. Rather, just as that old man turned from a human being into a watch in order for life to become bearable, my watch decided to turn from a watch into a human being.

In Palestine, it often stops moving. It suddenly enters into a coma, with which it becomes unable to count the time. On my last visit there, I set it as usual to local time the minute the plane touched down on the Lydd airport runway. It was ten to two in the afternoon. I headed to passport control. There weren't many travellers and the line I stood in was proceeding quickly. I handed my passport over to the police officer, and she took her time looking at it. Then more time. Suddenly, two men and a woman appeared, who were a mix of police, security and secret service, and they took me out of the line, so as to begin a long process of interrogation and searches. Everything proceeded as usual in such situations – an exhaustive interrogation into the smallest details of my life and a thorough search of my belongings. Afterwards I was led into a room to run a body search on me. And while a woman walked away with my shoes and belt to examine them by X-ray, another stayed with my watch, which she held inside her palms and went on contemplating with intent and sincerity. A few minutes later she looked at her watch, then back at my watch. Then again at her watch, then at my watch. When the first lady came back with the rest of my belongings, she hurried over to her to tell her that there was something strange about my watch. It was not moving. Five minutes had passed according to her watch, whereas according to mine none had passed. They called the security chief and my heart beat started to bang violently on my chest.

I didn't know how much time had passed before my watch, and then I were cleared of all suspicions and let go. But I discovered when I reached home that it was nine o'clock in the evening, while my watch was still pointing to ten to two in the afternoon. Maybe my watch was only trying to comfort me by making me believe that all that search and delay had lasted zero minutes. As if nothing had happened. Or perhaps it simply refuses to count the time that is seized from my life, a time whose only purpose is to humiliate me and send me into despair. A kind of time suspension, so as to obscure the time of pain.

Opposite to this malfunctioning in Palestine, my watch has not once stopped moving outside Palestine. It is never late to count every second of the other time. In fact, it many times moves slightly faster than it should, to a point where it seems to lose track of time. So fast it moves as if wanting to shake off this other time from it, one second after the other, so to catch up with the time in Palestine.

Thus, had it been seven hours or zero that distance my little watch from Palestine, it remains the same for it, and only to comfort me; it leads me out of time, no matter where I am.

ZUHEIR ABU SHAYEB

Martyr

they found him
luminous, green, in the field.
When they raise his hands
the grasses under them had turned to hearts.

It is said:
wheat stalks bloomed beneath his sleeves.
It is said:
the birds carried his blood
to his beloved cousins.
He shall return
Blossoming with volcanoes,
and fill again his mother's breasts.
When they found him green as light
they shrouded him with rose buds,
they spread out the sky to lay him on
and made the sun his pillow.

Translated by May Jayyusi and Naomi Shihab Nye

NAJWAN DARWISH

Nothing More to Lose

Lay your head on my chest and listen
To the layers of ruins
Behind the madrasah of saladin
Hear the houses sliced open
In the village of Lifta
Hear the wrecked mill, the lessons of reading
On the mosque's ground floor
Hear the balcony lights
Go out for the very last time
On the heights of Wadi Salib
Hear the crowds drag their feet
And hear them returning
Hear the bodies as they're thrown, listen
To their breathing on the bed
Of the Sea of Galilee
Listen like a fish
In a lake guarded by an angel
Hear the tales of the villagers, embroidered
Like kaffiyehs in the poems
Hear the singers growing old
Hear their ageless voices
Hear the women of Nazareth
As they cross the meadow
Hear the camel driver

Who never stops tormenting me
Hear it
And let us, together, remember
Then let us, together, forget
All that we have heard
Lay your head on my chest:
I'm listening to the dirt
I'm listening to the grass
As splits through my skin ...

We lost our heads in love
And have nothing more to lose

Translated by Kareem James Abu-Zeid

MAYA ABU AL-HAYYAT

Children

Whenever a child's hand comes out of a collapsed building
I check the hands of my three children
I count the digits of their hands and feet
I check the number of teeth
and the hairs of their eyebrows
Whenever a child's voice goes silent in Camp Al Yarmouk
I turn up the volume on the TV
and the songs on the radio
I pinch my three children on their sides
to keep them moving and feel they're alive
Whenever a heart is devoured by fear
on Qalandia checkpoint
I open my mouth and start to eat
Comfort myself with salty treats
Block out the sparks of the eyes that cry everywhere

Translated by Graham Fulton

I'm a Destitute Woman

Who lives on a checkpoint
Trivial things make me happy
Such as if my day passes without seeing a single bored soldier
I write my new novel there
About the butcher who wanted to become a violinist
Mad and evil
But his hand failed him
For a sharp, shiny knife
You know how bleak it is
To be alone and living on a checkpoint
Cheering for simple things
As if to transcend a chattering poet
And exhausted labourers carrying bags
Of bananas, guava and Tnuva milk
I'm a solitary woman
Who's lived in a grave for years
So far I haven't seen any demons or angels
But I definitely see a lot of bored soldiers

Translated by Maya Abu Al-Hayyat and Naomi Foyle

Return

Are we human beings?
The book with the yellow cover asks
We live in the designs and dreams of others,
In the way the wind has marked the trees thousands of years ago
Over the remains of animals, humans and scorpions
In the stomachs of whales, roots of trees and the echoes of nightly

conversations conducted by the inhabitants of caves
We wander in the streets of engineers and the ruins of
sharp shovels
in the plans of old municipalities and inside the mind of a reckless
old man
Our talk about the free soul, beliefs and the innocent land
is part of the design
One screw in the mind of a rocking chair
Giving the universe an outburst of passion

Return
They have written thousands of letters
Hung them on washing lines
To dry their ink and blood,
and when the wind came
followed its usual habit
digging and trimming
transferring letters and limbs
left traces of its own distorted load
Thus every time they searched in their memories for a road
An orange
Or an olive
Or a look from a window
They did not find it
That's how myths were made
Digging and trimming
Drip by drip
Bitterly dragging the memory
You do not know
How bitter it is
to search in the map for a memory
and find its corpse still fresh ...

Translated by Atef Alshaer

REMI KANAZI

Nakba

she was scared
seven months pregnant
guns pointed at temples
tears dropping
stomach cusped
back bent
dirt pathways
leading to
dispossession

rocking boats
waves crashing
people rushing
falling over each other
packing into small spaces
like memories

her home
mandated
occupied
cleansed
conquered

terrorisers

sat on hills
sniping children
neighbours fled
on April 10
word came
of massacre

didn't fight
didn't leave
shells and bombs
bursting in air
like anthems

prayed for the dead
with priests and imams
prayed for the living
looking over shoulders
for the Irgun and Haganah

a warrior
raised life
planted trees
painted fruit
cared for the road
as if it was her garden

orphaned twice
after birth
from Palestine
whispered Yaffa
till final breath
never knew essence

until she found
emptiness

48 ways to flee
and she found Beirut
bullet holes in buildings
reminder of home
but not home

years later
daughters sat
on hills in the South
dreaming of breaking
water never touched

thinking of their mother
that warrior
how battles still
raged here and abroad

orchards flourished
propagandists called
them barren
land expropriated
for Europeans
thirsting for
territory

colonist
non-native
not from here
plant flags, call it home

rename cities and villages
uprooting graveyards
wiping/clearing/cleansing
memory that this
is not theirs

passed away
August 22, 2009
frail hands shook
lip trembled
didn't want to die
but suffered decades

she spoke in Arabic
broken English
wounded words
and murmurs
her eyes closed
but every so often
they blinked brilliance
memories that could not
be erased, uprooted
or cleansed

she had not forgotten
we have not forgotten
we will not forget
veins like roots
of olive trees

we will return
that is not a threat

not a wish
a hope
or a dream
but a promise

A Poem for Gaza

I never knew death
until I saw the bombing
of a refugee camp
craters
filled with
dismembered legs
and splattered torsos
but no sign of a face
the only impression
a fading scream

I never understood pain
until a seven-year-old girl
clutched my hand
stared up at me
with soft brown eyes
waiting for answers

I didn't have any
I had muted breath
and dry pens in my back pocket
that couldn't fill pages
of understanding or resolution

in her other hand
she held a key
to her grandmother's house
but I couldn't unlock the cell
that caged her older brothers
they said:
we slingshot dreams
so the other side
will feel our father's presence!

a craftsman
built homes in areas
where no one was building

when he fell
silence

a .50 calibre bullet
tore through his neck
shredding his vocal cords
too close to the wall
his hammer
must have been a weapon
he must have been a weapon
encroaching on settlement hills
and demographics

so his daughter
studies mathematics

seven explosions
times

eight bodies
equals
four congressional resolutions

seven Apache helicopters
times
eight Palestinian villages
equals
silence and a second Nakba

our birthrate
minus
their birthrate
equals
one sea and 400 villages re-erected

one state
plus
two peoples
... and she can't stop crying

never knew revolution
or the proper equation
tears at the paper
with her fingertips
searching for answers
but only has teachers
looks up to the sky
to see Stars of David
demolishing squalor
with Hellfire missiles

she thinks back
words and memories
of his last hug
before he turned and fell
now she pumps
dirty water from wells
while settlements
divide and conquer
and her father's killer
sits beachfront
with European vernacular

this is our land!, she said
she's seven years old
this is our land!
she doesn't need history books
or a schoolroom teacher
she has these walls
this sky
her refugee camp

she doesn't know the proper equation
but she sees my dry pens
no longer waiting for my answers
just holding her grandmother's key
searching
for ink

TOUFIC HADDAD

Jiddo

seventy-nine years ago
my father's father
smiled

it was a boy
and he was the first

and as these things go
you smile
and thank god
give fenugreek sweets
to the mother
to strengthen
her blood

there,
across the street
he sat
a young father

'Toufic Khalil Haddad'
hung on his door

perhaps

I imagined him
cadastral maps
and compass
measuring
distances
between
here
and eternity

across the street
he looked out
to the cemetery ...

who knows what people think when
they look to cemeteries?

perhaps

during lunch
he'd walk through
find some shade
in the scent of the dry pine needles
to think
plan

how
he would build
on the plot
in Ard al-Hamra

how
the Mutran school fees

would be paid

how
he could avoid knowing then
what we all know now

* * *

spring sun
in Jerusalem
is exquisite

deceivingly

exquisite

and I close my eyes
and sigh

shake my head

* * *

when my father
finally told me
about the day

that spring day

when the car pulled up,
and the suitcases were put in

I understood
what he was doing

I understood
about the graveyard
and the breath
you breathe
when
things you should have known
are finally known

* * *

every life
has a story
or so they say

and I
never knew
yours

jiddo

it was there
buried
in a shallow grave
with no flowers

that horrible
anonymous way
precious
things
crush

and disappear

I would like to believe
there is a transcript

where
everything
is written

and everything returns

and all wounds sewn shut
heal
even if they scar

because small things matter

but I am
too old
for stories

and history,
too long
for
exception

there are only
graves

graves you must find
graves you must mind

ATEF ABU SAIF

Excerpt from The Drone Eats with Me

The worst thing is when you realise you no longer understand what's going on. Through the night, the tanks, drones, F16s, and warships haven't let up for a single minute. The explosions are constant, always sounding like they're just next door. Sometimes you're convinced that they're in your every room, that you've finally been hit. Then you realise, another miss: My mobile has run out of battery so I'm unable to listen to the news. Instead I lie in the dark and guess what's going on, make up my own analysis.

In time, you start to distinguish between the different types of attack. By far, the easiest distinction you learn to make is between an air attack, a tank attack and an attack from the sea. The shells coming in from the sea are the largest in size, and the boom they make is much deeper than anything else you hear. It's an all-engulfing, all-encompassing kind of sound; you feel like the ground itself is being swallowed up. Tank rockets, by comparison, give off a much hollower sound. Their explosions leave more of an echo in the air but you don't feel it so much from beneath. In contrast, a rocket dropped from an F16 produces an unmistakable, brilliant white light as well as a long reverberation. A bomb from an F16 makes the whole street dance a little for a good thirty seconds or so. You feel you might have to jump out of the window any minute to escape the building's collapse. Different from all these, though, is the rocket from a drone. This rocket seems to have more personality – it projects a sharp yellow light into the sky. A few seconds before a drone strike, this bright light spreads over the sky as if the rocket is telling us: 'It's dinner time, time to feast.'

These are just impressions, of course. But impressions are what enable you to process the strange array of details you're given. None of the attributes I am assigning to these rockets may be true. In reality, I might be exaggerating the differences or imagining them completely. But when you sit each night in your living room, waiting for death to knock at your door or send you a text message, telling you 'death's coming in sixty seconds', when you look for your future and see only the unknown, when you are unable to answer the one question your kids need an answer to ('when is it going to end, Dad?'), when you struggle to summon the strength you need each day, just to get through that day ... in these situations, which are, of course, all the same situation, what else can you do but form 'impressions.'

Tonight, we spend the whole night, until 5 a.m., surrounded by this orchestra of explosions, trying to make sense of it. At 5.30 a.m., my father-in-law comes in from the mosque and shares the news he's picked up from the people attending the dawn prayer. Five members of the Abu Aytah family were killed while sleeping, just two hours ago. They had sought safety on the ground floor of their building, thinking that the physics of an F16 rocket would abide by their logic. With no warning, the rocket converted them into fragments. Elsewhere, tanks are now approaching Jabalia, our district, from the east, a region known as Ezbet Abed Rabbo.

The war has divided the Strip into portions, separate courses if you like, and the Lord of War is eating them one course at a time, savouring each one. When the war started three weeks ago, back when it was just air strikes, Shuja'iyya became the first course, with more than 120 killed and some 700 injured (a number that changes daily, of course, as more bodies are uncovered, more survivors pulled out of the rubble). After that, the Lord of War decided he fancied a different piece of the Gaza-cake, and moved towards Beit Hanoun. The same sort of massacre took place there, the same sort of mass exodus, only with different human ingredients. Then, three days ago, the focus shifted to Khuza'a, near Khan Younis. Thousands were displaced. Yesterday some fifty people were killed in Khuza'a alone.

Last night, the tanks approached Ezbet Abed Rabbo, which is just one kilometre from where we're staying. Tank shells fell around us all day long. Most of the people have already left their homes over there. In the 2008–2009 war, a famous massacre was committed in Ezbet Abed Rabbo that has since been acknowledged in the UN's Goldstone Report. Everything was destroyed. Not a single house survived the destruction. Corpses remained under the rubble for a week.

The night before last, an F16 rocket struck two streets behind us. War teaches you how to adapt to its logic but it doesn't share its biggest secret, of course: how to survive it. For instance, whenever there's a war on you have to leave your windows half open so the pressure from the blasts does not blow them out. To be even safer, you should cover every pane of the window with adhesive tape so that, when it does break, the shards don't fly indoors or fall on people in the street below. It goes without saying you should never sleep anywhere near a window. The best place to sleep, people say, is near the stairs, preferably under them – that part of a building is structurally strongest. The shell that fell two nights ago landed 150 metres away. The first thing you do in the seconds afterwards, once you've checked on your loved ones, is inspect the damage. Usually it's just windows and doors. This shell, it turned out, landed smack in the middle of the Jabalia cemetery. The dead do not fight wars, by and large, they're too busy being dead, but on this occasion they were forced to participate in the suffering of the living. The next morning, dirty, grey bones lay scattered about the broken gravestones. At the moment of impact, these old corpses must have flown upwards into the air. I think about this moment. I wonder what might have happened to the spirits of these corpses in that split second of flight, what they must have made of the living occupants of Gaza, sitting patiently in their living rooms, praying for survival.

GHAYATH ALMADHOUN

Schizophrenia

I think of Palestine, the country that invented God, thus causing the bloodshed of millions of souls in the name of God. This is the country of milk and honey, where there is neither milk nor honey. This is the holy land, because of which we have waged holy wars; and we were dealt holy defeats; we were expelled by a holy expulsion, and we lived in holy refugee camps, and we died a holy death. I think of it, and then the voice of the sheikh who every time I asked, repeated one verse from the Qur'an, 'O believers, do not ask about things which if you knew about, would trouble you.' I still ask: 'Which is more distant from the earth? The planet of Jupiter? Or the two state-solution? Which is nearer to my soul? A solider from my country? Or a poet from my enemy? Which is the worst thing that Alfred Nobel did? The dynamite or the Nobel Prize?'

Translated by Atef Alshaer

How I Became ...

Her grief fell from the balcony and broke into pieces, so she needed a new grief. When I went with her to the market the prices were unreal, so I advised her to buy a used grief. We found one in excellent condition although it was a bit big. As the vendor told us, it belonged to a young poet who had killed himself the previous summer. She liked this grief so we decided to take it. We argued with the vendor over the price and he said he'd give us an angst dating from the sixties as a free gift if we bought the grief. We agreed, and I was happy with this unexpected angst. She sensed this and said, 'It's yours.' I took it and put it in my bag and we went off. In the evening I remembered it and took it out of the bag and examined it closely. It was high quality and in excellent condition despite half a century of use. The vendor must have been unaware of its value otherwise he wouldn't have given it to us in exchange for buying a young poet's low-quality grief. The thing that pleased me most about it was that it was existentialist angst, meticulously crafted and containing details of extraordinary subtlety and beauty. It must have belonged to an intellectual with encyclopaedic knowledge or a former prisoner. I began to use it and insomnia became my constant companion. I became an enthusiastic supporter of peace negotiations and stopped visiting relatives. There were increasing numbers of memoirs in my bookshelves and I no longer voiced my opinion, except on rare occasions. Human beings became more precious to me than nations and I began to feel a general ennui, but what I noticed most was that I had become a poet.

Massacre

Massacre is a dead metaphor that is eating my friends, eating them without salt. They were poets and have become Reporters With Borders; they were already tired and now they're even more tired. 'They cross the bridge at daybreak fleet of foot' and die with no phone coverage. I see them through night-vision goggles and follow the heat of their bodies in the darkness; there they are, fleeing from it even as they run towards it, surrendering to this huge massage. Massacre is their true mother, while genocide is no more than a classical poem written by intellectual pensioned-off generals. Genocide isn't appropriate for my friends, as it's an organised collective action and organised collective actions remind them of the Left that let them down.

Massacre wakes up early, bathes my friends in cold water and blood, washes their underclothes and makes them bread and tea, then teaches them a little about the hunt. Massacre is more compassionate to my friends than the Universal Declaration of Human Rights. Massacre opened the door to them when other doors were closed, and called them by their names when news reports were looking for numbers. Massacre is the only one to grant them asylum regardless of their backgrounds; their economic circumstances don't bother Massacre, nor does Massacre care whether they are intellectuals or poets, Massacre looks at things from a neutral angle; Massacre has the same dead features as them, the same names as their widowed wives, passes like them through the countryside and the suburbs and appears suddenly like them in breaking news. Massacre resembles my friends, but always arrives before them in faraway villages and children's schools.

Massacre is a dead metaphor that comes out of the television and eats my friends without a single pinch of salt.

Both translated by Catherine Cobham

ASHRAF FAYADH

Being a Refugee

Being a Refugee means standing at the end of the line
to get a fraction of a country.
standing is something your grandfather did, without knowing the reason.
and the fraction is you.
Country: a card you put in your wallet with your money.
Money: pieces of paper with pictures of leaders.
Pictures: they stand in for you until your return.
Return: a mythical creature that appears in your grandfather's stories.
Here ended the first lesson.
The lesson is conveyed to you so that you can learn the second lesson, which is
'what do you signify?'

Translated by Mona Kareem and Jonathan Wright

The Last of the Line of Refugee Descendants

You give the world indigestion, and other problems, too.
Do not force the ground to vomit,
And stay close to it, very close.
A fracture that can't be set,
A fraction that can't be resolved
Or added to the other numbers,
You cause some confusion in global statistics.

We are actors without getting paid. Our role is to stand as naked as when our mothers gave birth to us, as when the Earth gave birth to us, as the news bulletins gave birth to us, and the multi-page reports, and the villages that border on settlements, and the keys my grandfather carries. My poor grandfather, he did not know that the locks had changed. My grandfather, may the doors that open with digital cards curse you and may the sewage water that runs past your grave curse you. May the sky curse you, and not rain. Never mind, your bones can't grow from under the soil, so the soil is the reason we don't grow again.

Granddad, I'll stand for you on the Day of Judgment, because my private parts are no strangers to the Camera.

Do they allow filming on the Day of Judgment?

* * *

Granddad, I stand naked every day without any judgement, without anyone needing to be any last trumpet, because I have been sent on in advance. I am Hell's experiment on planet Earth.

The Hell that has been prepared for Refugees.

Translated by Jonathan Wright

Cracked Skin

My country passed through here
Wearing the freedom shoe.
It went far away, leaving its shoe behind.
It was running in a confused rhythm, like the beat of my heart.
My heart, which was running in another direction, with no convincing reason!
The freedom shoe was torn, old and fake,
Like human values in all their dimensions.
Everything left me behind and went away including you.
The shoe is a confusing invention.
It proves our ineligibility to live on this planet.
It proves we belong to another place, where we do not need to walk for long,
Maybe its floor is paved with cheap slippery ceramics.
The problem is not with slipperiness, but with water.
The problem of heat, broken glass, thorns, dry branches, pointed rocks.
The shoe is not an ideal solution ...
But it satisfies certain of our purposes,
Exactly like the mind,
Like emotion.
My emotion is dead since you left me last time.
I cannot reach you since my imprisonment
inside a cement box engraved with cold metal rods.
Since everyone forgot me, starting with my freedom,
ending with my shoes which suffer from an identity crisis.

Translated by Waleed Al-Bazoon and Naomi Foyle

DAREEN TATOUR

Resist, My People, Resist Them

Resist, my people, resist them.
In Jerusalem, I dressed my wounds and breathed my sorrows,
And carried the soul in my palm
For an Arab Palestine.
I will not succumb to the 'peaceful solution',
Never lower my flags
Until I evict them from my land.
I cast them aside for a coming time.
Resist, my people, resist them.
Resist the settlers' robbery
And follow the caravan of martyrs.
Shred the disgraceful constitution
Which imposed degradation and humiliation
And deterred us from restoring justice.
They burned blameless children;
As for Hadil, they sniped her in public,
Killed her in broad daylight.
Resist, my people, resist them.
Resist the colonialist's onslaught.
Pay no mind to his agents among us
Who chain us with the peaceful illusion.
Do not fear doubtful tongues;
The truth in your heart is stronger;
As long as you resist in a land

That has lived through raids and victory.
So Ali called from his grave:
Resist, my rebellious people-
Write me as prose on the agarwood;
My remains have you as a response.
Resist, my people, resist them.
Resist, my people, resist them.

A Poet Behind Bars

Jelemeh Prison, 2 November 2015 (the day I was indicted)

In prison, I met people
too numerous to count:
Killer and criminal,
thief and liar,
the honest and those who disbelieve,
the lost and confused,
the wretched and the hungry.
Then, the sick of my homeland,
born out of pain,
refused to comply with injustice
until they became children whose innocence was violated.
The world's compulsion left them stunned.
They grew older.
No, their sadness grew,
strengthening in repression,
like roses in salted soil.
They embraced love without fear,
and were condemned, not
for their deeds, but for declaring,
'We love the land endlessly,'

so their love freed them.
See, prison is for lovers.
I interrogated my soul
during moments of doubt and distraction:
'What of your crime?'
Its meaning escapes me now.
I said the thing and
revealed my thoughts;
I wrote about the current injustice,
wishes in ink,
a poem I wrote ...
The charge has worn my body,
from my toes to the top of my head,
for I am a poet in prison,
a poet in the land of art.
I am accused of words,
my pen the instrument.
Ink – blood of the heart – bears witness
and reads the charges.
Listen, my destiny, my life,
to what the judge said:
A poem stands accused,
my poem morphs into a crime.
In the land of freedom,
the artist's fate is prison.

Both translated by Tariq Haydar

AMIRA SAKALLA

Poetry of Resistance

Do not be ashamed
at the persistence of your tears.
Do not question
how they flow.

Do not look around
at the stale faces of others.
Asking how
they do not know.

You are not like them,
especially when
you cry.

For when you cry,
your tears are not yours alone.
When you cry,
you cry the tears
of your ancestors.

Palestine from the Sky

I don't want to be here
confined in this body
where the passage of time
is my most
intimate
partner.

All else is exile.
All else is a flattened landscape.
Crushed down,
unearthed,
swept off.

and I must build again.
I must build again.

I don't want to f*cking be here
inside my body
absorbing
so many hits as the winds
of time strike hard
on my limbs and leave
me rathering that I be broken
into pieces
and
dis-
solved
into sand
because
at least the sand all moves in the same direction

when the wind blows.

I want to escape my body and
go where the souls go and know
that they got to return and know
that they got to fly and know
that they got to know that I loved them
before I knew.

I don't want to be here
in my body because the body is a strong thing
that protects the soul from damage
and who says I deserve that?
Who said what souls should leave
their bodies so soon.

I ran across continents looking for my home
and in my exile I concluded that it is only
my body but my heart and soul
want to fly free,
not subjected to the pain of my body.

When will I finally blossom
When will I finally bloom
for the world to see
When will the birds
sing lines of my poetry?

I hate the journey.
I hate the path.
I'm sorry, prophets of God,
that I'd say that.

But who deserves to arrive
if Yaser[1] could never
see Palestine
from the sky.

We Weren't Supposed to Survive But We Did

We weren't supposed to survive but we did.
We weren't supposed to remember but we did.
We weren't supposed to write but we did.
We weren't supposed to fight but we did.
We weren't supposed to organise but we did.
We weren't supposed to rap but we did.
We weren't supposed to find allies but we did.
We weren't supposed to grow communities but we did.
We weren't supposed to return but WE ARE.

1 Yaser Murtaja was a Palestinian journalist. He was killed by the Israeli army while covering protests at the edge of the Gaza strip on 6 April 2018.

ABOUT THE CONTRIBUTORS

Maya Abu Al-Hayyat (1980–)
Maya Abu Al-Hayyat is a published author of novels, short stories and poetry collections. She was born in Lebanon and completed her BSc degree in Civil Engineering at Al-Najah University. In 2005, she was awarded the Young Creative Writer Award by the Ministry of Culture, followed with the Young Writer Award for Poetry from the AM Qattan Foundation in 2006. Her short story for children, *The Red Bird*, was translated into English in 2011.

Atef Abu Saif (1973–)
Atef Abu Saif was born in the Jabalia refugee camp in the Gaza Strip in 1973. He is the author of four novels, *Shadows in the Memory, The Tale of the Harvest Night, Snowball* and *The Salty Grape of Paradise*; the memoir *The Drone Eats with Me*; a short story collection *Everything is Normal*; and the editor of the short story anthology *The Book of Gaza*. He is a regular contributor to several Palestinian and Arabic newspapers and journals and has a PhD in Political and Social Sciences from the European University Institute in Florence.

Zuheir Abu Shayeb (1958–)
Zuheir Abu Shayeb was born in the village of Deir Ghusun. He obtained a BA in Arabic Literature from Jordan's Yarmouk University in 1983, and has worked as a teacher, graphic designer and an art critic. The author of several poetry collections, he currently lives and works in Amman as Art Director of Muassassah al-Arabiyya al-Dirassat wal-Nashr.

Salman Abu Sitta (1937–)
Salman Abu Sitta is a renowned researcher on and spokesperson for refugee affairs. He is Founder and President of the Palestine Land Society and General Coordinator of the Right of Return Congress, and

has served as a member of the Palestine National Council. He comes from a village that bore his family name, the Abu Sitta spring well, in Beer Sheba District of Palestine, and as a boy became a refugee in the Gaza Strip. He received a PhD in Civil Engineering from University College London. His acclaimed autobiography *Mapping My Return: A Palestinian Memoire* was published in 2016.

Taha Muhammad Ali (1931–2011)
Taha Muhammad Ali was born in the village of Saffuriyya, Galilee. An autodidact, he owned a souvenir shop now run by his sons near Nazareth's Church of the Annunciation. He published several collections of poetry and a volume of short stories.

Hanan Ashrawi (1946–)
Hanan Ashrawi is a Palestinian legislator, activist and academic. After receiving a PhD in Medieval and Comparative Literature from the University of Virginia, Dr Ashrawi returned to Palestine and established the Department of English at Birzeit University in the West Bank in 1978. She is the author of *The Modern Palestinian Short Story: An Introduction to Practical Criticism*; *Contemporary Palestinian Literature under Occupation*; *Contemporary Palestinian Poetry and Fiction*; and *Literary Translation: Theory and Practice*, and the editor of *The Anthology of Palestinian Literature.*

Samira Azzam (1927–1967)
Samira Azzam was a Palestinian writer, teacher, broadcaster and translator. She began publishing her stories in periodicals as a teenager under the *nom de plume* 'Girl of the Coast'. She fled to Lebanon with her family in 1948 before moving to Iraq where she became the headmistress of a girls' school and radio broadcaster for the Near East Asia Broadcasting Company. Azzam's first set of short stories, *Small Things*, was published in 1954. She published two further short story collections.

Liana Badr (1950–)
Liana Badr was born in Jerusalem and raised in Jericho. She is a

prize-winning film writer and director, and the author of novels, short stories, poetry collections and children's books, which have been translated into several languages. Badr runs the Cinema and Audiovisual Department at the Palestinian Ministry of Culture in Ramallah. She has worked as a volunteer in various women's organisations and as a field reporter and editor of the cultural section of *Al Hurriyya*. She is the founding editor of the periodical *Dafater Thaqafiyya*.

Ramzy Baroud (1972–)
Ramzy Baroud is an Palestinian-American journalist, media consultant, author and internationally-syndicated columnist. He is the editor of *Palestine Chronicle*, the former managing editor of *Middle East Eye* and the former deputy managing editor of Al Jazeera online. He is the author of four books, including *The Last Earth: A Palestinian Story*, which have been translated into several languages. Baroud has a PhD in Palestine Studies from the University of Exeter and is a Non-Resident Scholar at Orfalea Center for Global and International Studies, University of California Santa Barbara.

Muin Bseiso (1926–1984)
Muin Besiso was a prominent poet and writer with a prolific output. Born in Gaza, he started publishing his poetry in the Jaffa-based magazine *al-Hurriya*. He studied at the American University of Cairo and was imprisoned in Egyptian jails twice, 1955–1957 and 1959–1963. He became a member of the Communist Party in Gaza and a notable member of the Palestinian National Council. His writing includes several poetry collections such as *The Traveller* and *When Stones Rain*; plays including *The Tragedy of Che Guvera, The Revolution of the Blacks* and *The Rock*; and numerous prose works and articles.

Selma Dabbagh (1970–)
Selma Dabbagh is a British-Palestinian writer of fiction. Her first novel, *Out of It*, was a *Guardian* Book of the Year. It has been translated into Arabic, French and Italian. In 2014, her play set in

Jerusalem, *The Brick*, was produced by BBC Radio 4 and nominated for an Imison Award. She has written for *The Guardian*, *The London Review of Books*, *GQ* and other publications and is currently working on her second novel and a film project.

Ahmad Dahbour (1946–2017)
Ahmad Dahbour was one of Palestine's most celebrated poets. Born in Haifa, his family fled to Lebanon in 1948, eventually settling in a refugee camp in Homs, Syria. Though he didn't complete high school education, Dahbour was an avid reader and published his first collection of poetry at eighteen. He went onto publish twelve further collections. Dahbour was the editor of *Lotus* magazine, editor-in-chief of *Albayadir*, general director of the Culture Department of the Palestinian Liberation Organisation and Deputy Minister of Culture of the Palestinian Authority. He was presented with the Tawfiq Zayyad Poetry Award in 1988, the Medal of the Order of Merit and Superiority by Mahmoud Abbas in 2012, and the Jerusalem Award for Culture and Creativity in 2015.

Mahmoud Darwish (1941–2008)
Mahmoud Darwish was born in the village of al-Birweh in the Galilee in Palestine. He became a refugee at age seven. He worked as a journalist and editor in Haifa and left to study in Moscow in 1970. His exilic journey took him to Cairo, Beirut, Tunis, Paris, Amman and Ramallah, where he settled in 1995. He is one of the most celebrated and revered poets in the Arab world. He published more than thirty books, and his poetry has been translated into thirty-five languages. Darwish was named a Knight of the Order of Arts and Letters by France in 1993, was awarded the Lannan Cultural Freedom Prize in 2001, the Prince Claus Award in 2004, and the Cairo Prize for Arabic Poetry in 2007.

Najwan Darwish (1978–)
Najwan Darwish is a poet, journalist, editor and cultural critic from Jerusalem. Described by the *New York Review of Books* as 'one of the foremost Arabic-language poets of his generation', his poetry

has been translated into over twenty languages. Hay Festival Beirut selected him as one of the thirty-nine best Arab writers under the age of forty and, in 2014, NPR listed his work *Nothing More to Lose* as one of the best books of the year. He is Chief Editor of the culture section of *Al Araby Al Jadeed* newspaper and is a literary advisor for the Palestine Festival of Literature.

Sharif S. Elmusa (1947–)

Sharif S. Elmusa is a poet, academic and translator of Arabic poetry and fiction. His poems and essays have appeared in *The Massachusetts Review, Mizna, The Indian Quarterly, Jadaliyya* and in his poetry collection *Flawed Landscapes.* He is the co-editor of *Grape Leaves: A Century of Arab-American Poetry*. Elmusa was Associate Professor of Political Science at the American University in Cairo, and taught at Georgetown University, Qatar, and Yale University.

Ashraf Fayadh (1980–)

Ashraf Fayadh is an artist and poet, born in Saudi Arabia to Palestinian parents. In November 2015 he was sentenced to death by beheading on the charge of apostasy. The Saudi Court overturned the sentence three months later and imposed an eight-year prison term with eight hundred lashes. Several international organisations, including English Pen and Human Rights Watch, have condemned his harsh imprisonment and sentence.

Emile Habibi (1922–1996)

Emile Habibi was born in Haifa. In 1943, he became secretary of the Palestinian Communist Party. He was a prominent member of the League of Arab Intellectuals and a founder of the National Liberation League in Palestine. Habibi represented the Israeli Communist Party in the Knesset between 1952 and 1972. He received wide renown with his second novel *The Secret Life of Saeed the Pessoptimist,* which was translated into sixteen languages. Habibi was the recipient of numerous prizes, including the Israel Prize in Literature. In 1991 he was selected as the most important author in the Arab world by *al-Majalla* magazine.

Toufic Haddad (1975–)

Toufic Haddad is a Palestinian-American writer, whose publications include *Palestine Ltd.: Neoliberalism and Nationalism in the Occupied Territory* and *Between the Lines: Israel, the Palestinians and the US War on Terror* (co-author). He holds a PhD from SOAS, University of London, and has previously worked as a journalist, editor and researcher in Jerusalem, including for different UN bodies.

Nathalie Handal (1969–)

Nathalie Handal is a French-American poet, playwright, translator and editor of Palestinian descent. Her poetry collections include *Love and Strange Horses*, winner of the Gold Medal Independent Publisher Book Award, and *Poet in Andalucía*. She has been playwright-in-residence at the New York Theatre Workshop, and her most recent plays have been produced at the John F. Kennedy Center for the Performing Arts, the Bush Theatre and Westminster Abbey in London. Handal teaches at Columbia University and at the Low-Residency MFA program at Sierra Nevada College and writes the literary travel column 'The City and the Writer' for *Words Without Borders*.

Rashid Hussein (1936–1977)

Rashid Hussein was born in the village of Musmus in Umm al-Fahim, Palestine. He worked as a teacher but was dismissed for his political activism. He wrote articles for various publications and poetry. He also translated a number of poems from Hebrew into Arabic including that of the Israeli Jewish poet Haim Nahman Bialik. Hussein was posthumously awarded the Order of Jerusalem for Culture and Art by the Palestinian Authority.

Jabra Ibrahim Jabra (1920–1994)

Jabra Ibrahim Jabra was born in Bethlehem. In 1939 he won a scholarship to study English literature at Cambridge University, UK. Jabra taught English literature in Jerusalem and later, Baghdad. He won many distinguished awards throughout his lifetime as well as a research fellowship at Harvard University, USA. Jabra was an intellectual and artist of many talents. He founded the Baghdad Group for Contemporary Art, held the post of editor in chief of the *Arab Art Magazine* and served as President of the Association of Art Critics in Iraq. He wrote short stories, poetry, essays, plays, literary criticism and novels and was also a highly accomplished translator. His own works have been translated into English, French, German and Italian.

Salma Khadra Jayyusi (1926–)

Salma Khadra Jayyusi was born in Safed, Palestine. She is prodigiously active as a poet, writer, translator and anthologist. She has lectured widely on Arabic literature and was the founder and director of PROTA (a pioneering project of translation from Arabic). She is renowned for several works including a two-volume critical history *Trends and Movements in Modern Arabic Poetry*; *Modern Arabic Fiction: An Anthology of Modern Arabic Poetry* and *An Anthology of Modern Palestinian Literature.*

Fady Joudah (1971–)

Fady Joudah is a Palestinian-American physician, poet and translator. He was born in Austin, Texas, and grew up in Libya and Saudi Arabia. Joudah's debut collection of poetry, *The Earth in the Attic*, won the 2007 Yale Series of Younger Poets. His other collections include *Alight, Textu* and *Footnotes in the Order of Disappearance.* Joudah was a Guggenheim Fellow in poetry in 2014. Joudah also translated poetry including *The Butterfly's Burden*, which won the Banipal Prize and was a finalist for the PEN Award for Poetry in Translation; and *If I Were Another*, which won a PEN USA Award, by Mahmoud Darwish. His translation of Ghassan Zaqtan's *Like a Straw Bird It Follows Me* won the Griffin International Poetry Prize in 2013.

Salem Jubran (1941–2011)

Salem Jubran was born in al-Buqai'a in upper Galilee and studied English literature and Middle Eastern History at the University of Haifa. In 1962 he joined Rakah, the Israeli Communist Party, and worked at *al-Ittihad*, the party's periodical. He later edited the journal *al-Ghad* and also wrote for several newspapers outlets in Israel and elsewhere, including the Lebanese paper *al-Nahar*. He published three poetry collections during his lifetime.

Ghassan Kanafani (1936–1972)

Ghassan Kanafani was born in Acre and fled to Damascus in 1948 with his family. Alongside his career as a writer, journalist, editor and playwright, Kanafani was spokesman and a leading member of the Popular Front for the Liberation of Palestine. Kanafani was prolific across a variety of written forms, from novels to short stories, literary researches and political essays. His fiction, which frequently portrays the complex dilemmas Palestinians must face, is known for its lucidity and clarity of expression. His novellas include *Men in the Sun* and *Returning to Haifa*. Kanafani was assassinated along with his niece Lamees after a bomb was planted under his car. He is buried at the Shuhada Cemetery, Jerusalem.

Remi Kanazi (1981–)

Remi Kanazi is a Palestinian-American performance poet, writer and organiser based in New York City. He is the editor of the anthology of hip hop, poetry and art, *Poets for Palestine*, and the author of two collections of poetry, *Poetic Injustice: Writings on Resistance and Palestine* and *Before the Next Bomb Drops: Rising Up from Brooklyn to Palestine*. His political commentary has been featured by news outlets throughout the world, including the *New York Times, Salon, Al Jazeera English* and the BBC. He is a Lannan Residency Fellow and is on the advisory committee for the Palestinian Campaign for the Academic and Cultural Boycott of Israel.

Abdelkarim al-Karmi (1907–1980)

Abdelkarim al-Karmi, also known as Abu Salma, was a Palestinian poet. He was born in Haifa and practised law until April 1948, when the Israelis occupied the city. He moved briefly to Acre, then to Damascus. Al-Karmi kept the keys to his house and office in Haifa all of his life, hoping to return one day. Much of al-Karmi's writing is concerned with his yearning for Palestine. He was awarded the Lotas

International Reward for Literature in 1978 by the Association of Asian and African Writers and the title 'The Olive of Palestine' was also bestowed on him.

Ghada Karmi (1939–)
Ghada Karmi trained as a doctor in the UK and later gained a PhD in the history of Arabic medicine from the University of London. She worked in the health service and lectured widely on the Palestinian cause and the Arab world. She has been a formidable campaigner for Palestinian rights, highlighting the necessity of the right of return for Palestinian refugees. She has written several acclaimed books on Palestine, including her notable memoir, *In Search of Fatima*.

Sayed Kashua (1973–)
Sayed Kashua is the author of the novels *Dancing Arabs*, *Let It Be Morning*, which was shortlisted for the International IMPAC Dublin Literary Award, and *Exposure*, winner of the prestigious Bernstein Prize. He is a columnist for *Haaretz*, a regular contributor to the *New Yorker* and the creator of the popular, prize-winning sitcom, *Arab Labor*. Kashua has received numerous awards for his journalism including the Lessing Prize for Critic (Germany) and the SFJFF Freedom of Expression Award (USA). Born in Tira, he now lives in the United States and teaches at the University of Illinois.

Sahar Khalifeh (1941–)
Sahar Khalifeh was born in Nablus. She won a scholarship to study English literature at the University of North Carolina and went on to receive a doctorate in Women's Studies and American Literature from Iowa University. To date she has published nine novels, all of which are concerned with Palestinians under occupation. Her works have been translated into English, French, German and Hebrew. She has won a number of Arab and international prizes, including the Alberto Moravia Prize (Italy), the Cervantes Award Prize (Spain) and the Naguib Mahfouz Prize (Egypt).

Elias Khoury (1948–)
Elias Khoury is a Lebanese novelist, playwright and critic. He is the author of thirteen novels, four non-fiction books and three plays. In 2000, he was awarded the Prize of Palestine for his widely celebrated novel *Gate of the Sun*. He founded the journal *al-Karmel* with Mahmoud Darwish and currently works as the Editor-in-Chief of the cultural pages of the daily newspaper *An-Nahar*.

Ghayath al-Madhoun (1979–)
Ghayath al-Madhoun is a Palestinian poet born in Damascus now living in Sweden. He has published four collections of poetry, and his work has been translated into fourteen languages. He has won numerous prizes, including the Klas de Vylders Stipendiefond for immigrant writers (Sweden). He co-wrote *Till Damascus* with the Swedish poet Marie Silkeberg, which was included in the Swedish national broadsheet *Dagens Nyheter* critic's list for Best New Books and produced as a Radio Play for Swedish National Radio.

Raba'i al-Madhoun (1945–)
Raba'i al-Madhoun is a journalist and novelist. Born in al-Majdal, Palestine, he now lives and works in London as a writer and editor at the leading Arabic daily, *Asharq Al-Awsat*. Al-Madhoun's debut novel, *The Lady from Tel Aviv*, is a bestseller in the Arab world and was shortlisted for the International Prize for Arabic Fiction in 2010. Al-Madhoun won the International Prize for Arabic Fiction with his second novel, *Destinies: Concerto of the Holocaust and the Nakba*. His other works include *The Idiot of Khan Younis* and *The Taste of Separation*.

Abdelrahim Mahmoud (1913–1948)
Abdelrahim Mahmoud was born in 'Anabta, Tulkarm. He was a student of Ibrahim Tuqan and under Tuqan's tutelage became a professor of Arabic Literature at Al-Najah School. When the uprising against the British Mandate began, Mahmoud left his job and attended a military college in Iraq for three years. He returned to Palestine to fight against the Zionists where he died during what

became known as the Battle of the Tree near Al-Nasirah, Nazareth. Islam features heavily in Mahmoud's poetry. Four long poems are known to us. Two of them concern the Qur'an and two focus on the Prophet Muhammad.

Lisa Suhair Majaj (1960–)
Lisa Suhair Majaj is a Palestinian-American poet and academic. Born in Hawarden, Iowa, Majaj was raised in Jordan. She studied English literature at the American University of Beirut and received a PhD in American Culture from the University of Michigan. In 2001, she moved to Nicosia, Cyprus. Her poetry and essays have been widely published. In 2008, she was awarded the Del Sol Press Annual Poetry Prize for her poetry manuscript *Geographies of Light*. She has also co-edited three collections of essays on international women writers.

Izzuddin Manasra (1946–)
Izzuddin Manasra is a writer, academic and journalist, born in Hebron. He received a PhD in Slavic literature from the Bulgarian Academy of Science. He has worked as the director of Cultural Programs for Jordanian radio, the editor of *Palestinian Affairs* magazine and as a professor of Comparative Literature at Constantine University, Algeria. One of his main areas of interest has been reviving the style and themes of Canaanite poetry. He has been the Secretary General of the Arab Contemporary Literary Society since 1984.

Ibrahim Nasrallah (1954–)
Ibrahim Nasrallah is a poet, novelist, professor and photographer, born in Amman and raised in Palestinian refugee camps. He has published more than eleven novels and is the Vice President of Darat Al-Funoun, the most prominent art and cultural centre in Jordan. Nasrallah is also an activist for Palestinian rights. He climbed Mount Kilimanjaro with a group of Palestinian amputees, drawing attention to the cause through recounting the experience in his prize-winning novel *The Souls of Kilimanjaro*. His work has been translated into numerous languages including English, Italian and Danish, and won many awards, such as the International Prize for Arabic Fiction

for *The Second War of the Dog*, the Naguib Mahfouz Prize and the Tayseer School prize.

Naomi Shihab Nye (1952–)

Naomi Shihab Nye is a poet, songwriter and novelist born in St Louis, Missouri. Her father was a Palestinian refugee and her mother an American of German and Swiss descent. She has written numerous collections of poetry including *Different Ways to Pray, 19 Varieties of Gazelle, Red Suitcase* and *Is This Forever, Or What?*, and edited many more. She has also published an essay collection, *Never in a Hurry*, a young-adult novel, *Habibi,* and a picture book, *Lullaby Raft*. Nye is the recipient of numerous honours and awards including a Lavan Award, the Paterson Poetry Prize, the Carity Randall Prize and many Pushcart Prizes. From 2010–2015 she served as a Chancellor of the Academy of American Poets.

Samih al-Qassim (1939–2014)

Samih al-Qassim was born in Zarqa, Jordan. He was among the first of the Arab Druze to defy the compulsory military service imposed by the Israeli authorities. He became a teacher in Galilee but was dismissed from his post by the Israeli education minister. He found alternative employment as an assistant electrical welder, a gas station attendant and inspector in the Urban Planning Department in Nazareth. Al-Qassim edited both *al-Ittihad*, the organ of the Communist Party in Arabic and the cultural magazine *al-Jadid*. He also helped to establish Arabesque Publishing House, ran the Popular Arts Institute in Haifa and headed the Arab Writers Union in Israel. Al-Qassim published seventy books and won many awards, including the Jerusalem Medal for Culture, the Naguib Mahfouz Prize and the Palestine Prize for Poetry.

Edward Said (1935–2003)

Edward Said was a Palestinian-American academic, political activist and literary critic. He attended Princeton and Harvard Universities, where he specialised in English literature. He joined the faculty of Columbia University as a lecturer, and later became a professor. He was an outspoken proponent of the political rights of the Palestinian people. In 1978 Said published *Orientalism*, his best-known work and one of the most influential scholarly books of the twentieth century.

Amira Sakalla (1994–)
Amira Sakalla is a Palestinian activist. She founded Students for Justice in Palestine whilst studying at the University of Tennessee, studied Violence, Conflict and Development at the School of Oriental and African Studies, University of London, and has interned at If Americans Knew and Friends of Sabeel North America. She blogged about Palestine from her tumblr account 'Coffeeandslingshots', which has since been deleted, and now contributes articles to the likes of *Huffington Post* and *The New Arab*.

May Sayigh (1940–)
May Sayigh was born in 1940 in Gaza and studied Sociology and Philosophy at Cairo University. She was the president of the Union of Palestinian Women and has been very active in the cause of Palestinian women and liberation. She has published a number of poetry collections as well as a prose account of the 1982 Israeli invasion of Lebanon in *The Siege*. She lives in Paris.

Adania Shibli (1974–)
Adania Shibli has written novels, plays, short stories and narrative essays. She has twice been awarded the Qattan Young Writer's Award, once for her novel *Touch* and in 2003 for her novel *We Are All Equally Far from Love*. She is the editor of *Dispositions*, an art book about contemporary Palestinian artists. Shibli is a visiting professor at Birzeit University.

Dareen Tatour (1982–)
Dareen Tatour is a Palestinian poet and photographer, born in Reineh near Nazareth. She was arrested in 2015 in Israel over her published poem 'Resist, My People, Resist Them'. She was placed under house arrest, tried and convicted, and served a prison sentence over social media postings she made in Arabic on Youtube, Facebook

and her blog. She was released on 20 September 2018. Her debut collection of poetry *The Last Invasion* was published in 2010. Her latest collection of poems and a novel titled *An Appointment with the Whales* were ready for publication, but exist only on her laptop, which was confiscated by Israeli authorities.

Fadwa Tuqan (1917–2003)
Fadwa Tuqan was a poet from Nablus, and sister of Ibrahim Tuqan. She studied English literature at Oxford University and published eight poetry collections, which enjoyed renown throughout the Arab world. Selections of her poetry have been translated into English, French, German, Italian, Persian and Hebrew. Tuqan was elected to the Board of Trustees of al-Najah University when it was founded in 1977, wrote the university anthem and was granted an honorary doctorate. She won numerous prizes, including the annual Sulayman Arar Poetry Prize, the Prize of the Union of Jordanian Writers, the Sultan Uways Prize of the United Arab Emirates, the Prize of the World Festival of Contemporary Writing, the Tunisian Cultural Medal and the PLO Prize for literature.

Ibrahim Tuqan (1905–1941)
Ibrahim Tuqan was a poet and teacher of Arabic literature. In 1929 he began to compose nationalist poetry. He wrote of the land and criticised quarrels among Palestine's leaders. 'My Homeland', Tuqan's best-known ode, was put to music and became the unofficial anthem of Palestine and the Iraqi anthem after the US invasion in 2003. 'The Red Tuesday' was composed and recited in response to the 17 June 1930 executions of Fouad Hijazi, Muhammad Jamjoum and Atta al-Zeer. The PLO posthumously awarded Tuqan the Jerusalem Medal for Culture, Arts and Literature in January 1990.

Fawaz Turki (1941–)
Fawaz Turki was born in Haifa, Palestine. He is the author of a number of books, including *The Disinherited: Journal of a Palestinian Exile* and *Exile's Return: The Making of a Palestinian-American*, as well as several poetry collections. He has lectured around the country

and has been published extensively in the US. He has been a writer-in-residence at both SUNY Buffalo and the Virginia Center for the Creative Arts. He currently lives in Washington, DC.

Yahya Yakhlif (1944–)

Yahya Yakhlif was born in the village of Samakh near Lake Tiberias in Palestine. He was forced to move to Jordan with his family in 1948. He studied Arabic literature at the Arab University of Beirut, then joined the Palestinian National Movement and became a prominent member of its National Council, and eventually the Minister of Culture in the Palestinian Authority. He has written several collections of short stories and a number of novels, including *The Sky's Water*, which was nominated for the International Prize for Arabic Fiction.

Ghassan Zaqtan (1954–)

Ghassan Zaqtan is a writer, born near Bethlehem in Beit Jala and now living in Ramallah. He lived in Amman, Jordan, for twelve years where he qualified as a teacher. Critically acclaimed among avant-garde artists in the Arab world, he has published numerous poetry collections, including *The Silence That Remains*, and two novels. The English translation of his collection *Like a Straw Bird It Follows Me* won the 2013 Griffin International Poetry Prize.

Tawfiq Zayyad (1929–1994)

Tawfiq Zayyad was a Palestinian poet, writer, academic and politician. He was elected mayor of Nazareth and served as a member of the Israeli Knesset. He co-authored a report on Israeli prison conditions and the abuse of Palestinian inmates for the UN General Assembly report, where it was described as 'perhaps the best evidence of the truth of the reports describing the repugnant inhumane conditions endured by Arab prisoners'. Zayyad was allegedly targeted for assassination by the Israeli occupation. In addition to his translations of Russian literature and the work of the Turkish poet Nazem Hikmat, Zayyad published a number of collections of his own poems, including *I Press on Your Hands*.

CREDITS

We are grateful to the following copyright holders who have given us permission to reprint the selections found in this anthology.

Adania Shibli
'Out of Time' by Adania Shibli was first presented during the workshop 'The Politics of Images: Practices and Approaches to Art in the Middle East and North Africa; organised by documenta 12, on November 20th, 2006, in Bruno Kreisky Forum, Vienna.

Ahmad Dahbour
'New Suggestions' by Ahmad Dahbour, translated by A. M. Elmessiri (Palestine InSight, 29 December 2017).

Banipal
One Sky by Liana Badr, translated by Becki Maddock, was first published in *Banipal 57* (Autumn/Winter 2016). 'At a Train Station that Fell Off the Map' by Mahmoud Darwish, translated by Sinan Antoon, was first published in *Banipal 33* (Autumn/Winter 2008).

Beacon Press and Comma Press
Excerpt from *The Drone Eats with Me* by Atef Abu Seif, (US: Beacon Press, 2016. UK & Comm: Comma Press, 2015).

Bloomsbury Publishing Plc
Excerpt from *Out of It* © Selma Dabbagh 2012, (Bloomsbury Publishing Plc, 2012).

Columbia University Press
'Martyr' by Zuheir Abu Shayeb, translated by May Jayyusi and Naomi Shihab Nye; 'The Vinegar Cup' by Muin Bseiso, translated by May Jayyusi and Naomi Shihab Nye; 'Against' by Rashid Hussein,

translated by May Jayyusi and Naomi Shihab Nye; 'Refugee' by Salem Jubran, translated by Lena Jayyusi and Naomi Shihab Nye; 'We Will Return' by Abdelkarim Al-Karmi, translated by Sharif S. Elmusa and Naomi Shihab Nye; 'The Martyr', translated by Adib S. Kawar, and 'The Aqsa Mosque' translated by Salma K. Jayyusi and Trevor LeGassick, by Abdelrahim Mahmoud; 'Dawn Visitors' by Izzuddin Manasra, translated by May Jayyusi and Naomi Shihab Nye; 'Departure' by May Sayigh, translated by Lena Jayyusi and Naomi Shihab Nye; from *Anthology of Modern Palestinian Literature*, edited by Salma Khadra Jayyusi (Columbia University Press, 1995).

Copper Canyon Press
'To Our Land' by Mahmoud Darwish, translated by Fady Joudah from *The Butterfly's Burden* (Copper Canyon Press, 2006).

Darwish Foundation
'I Am from There' translated by A. Z. Foreman (Poems in Translation Blog, 2010); 'On This Earth' translated by Karim Abuawad (*As It Ought To Be* Magazine, 24 August 2010); 'Standing Before the Ruins of Al-Birweh' translated by Sinan Antoon from Darwish's posthumous collection, *La Uridu Li-Hadhihi al-Qasidati an Tantahi* (*I Don't Want This Poem to End*) (Riyad al-Rayyis, 2009), (*Jadaliyya*, 13 March 2011) by Mahmoud Darwish, reprinted here by kind permission of the Darwish Foundation.

Fadwa Tuqan
Excerpt from 'Call of the Land' by Fadwa Tuqan, translation © 2006 by Tania Tamari Nasir and Christopher Millis from *Wahsha: Moustalhama min Qanoon al Jathibiya* (Al Karmel 72-73, 2002 by arrangement with the estate of Fadwa Tuqan); 'Hamza' 'Labour Pains' and 'The Deluge and the Tree' by Fadwa Tuqan, translated by Tania Tamari Nasir and Christopher Millis (Al Karmel 72-73, 2002 by arrangement with the estate of Fadwa Tuqan).

Ghayath al-Madhoun
'How I Became', 'Massacre' and excerpt from 'Schizophrenia' by

Ghayath al-Madhoun, translated by Catherine Cobham from *Adrenalin* (Action Books, 2017).

Hanan Ashrawi
'From the Diary of an Almost-Four-Year-Old' by Hanan Ashrawi (Madaale.com); 'Hadeel's Song' by Hanan Ashrawi (Media Monitors Network, 11 November 2000).

Ibrahim Nasrallah
Excerpt from *Street Olives* by Ibrahim Nasrallah, translated by Johnathan Wright, published in Arabic as *Zaytuun al-Shawaari'* (Arab Scientific Publishers, 2002).

Interlink Books
'Flawed Landscape' and 'In the Refugee Camp' from *Flawed Landscape* by Sharif S. Elmusa (Interlink books, 2008). Excerpt from *The Secret Life of Saeed: The Pessoptimist* by Emile Habibi, translated by Salma K. Jayyusi and Trevor LeGassick (Interlink World Fiction Series, 2001). Excerpt from *Wild Thorns* by Sahar Khalifeh, translated by Trevor LeGassick and Elizabeth Fernea (US: Interlink Books, 2000. UK: Saqi Books, 2005).

Issa J. Boullata
'Without Roots' by Salma Khadra Jayyusi, from *Modern Arab Poets: 1950-1975* (Three Continents Press, 1967). 'My Homeland' and 'Red Tuesday' by Ibrahim Tuqan, from *Tradition and Modernity in Modern Arabic Literature*, translated and edited by Issa J. Boullata (University of Arkansas Press, 1997).

Lisa Suhair Majaj
'Fifty Years On / Stones in an Unfinished Wall' by Lisa Suhair Majaj, from *Geographies of Light*, (Del Sol Press, 2009).

Lynne Rienner Publishers
'No' by Muin Bseiso, translated by Abdul Wahab Al-Messiri; 'The Prison' by Ahmad Dahbour, translated by A. M. Elmessiri; 'On the

Trunk of an Olive Tree' by Tawfiq Zayyad, translated by Adel Wahhab Elmessiri; from *The Palestinian Wedding: A Bilingual Anthology of Contemporary Palestinian Resistance Poetry*, edited and translated by A. M. Elmessiri. (Boulder, Lynne Rienner Publishers, 2011. Reprint from Three Continents Press, Inc., 1982). Excerpt from *Hunters in a Narrow Street: A Novel* by Jabra Ibrahim Jabra (Three Continents Press, 1990). 'A Present for the Holiday' by Ghassan Kanafani, translated by Barbara Harlow, from *Palestine's Children: Returning to Haifa and Other Stories* (Lynne Rienner Publishers, 2000).

Maya Abu Al-Hayyat
'Children' by Maya Abu Al-Hayyat, translated by Graham Fulton from *A Bird is not a Stone: An Anthology of Contemporary Palestinian Poetry* edited by Henry Bell and Sarah Irving (Freight Books, 2014).

Naomi Shihab Nye
'Blood' and 'Different Ways to Pray' from *Words Under the Words: Selected Poems* by Naomi Shihab Nye (A Far Corner Book) (The Eighth Mountain Press, 1994); 'How Palestinians Keep Warm' from *Red Suitcase* by Naomi Shihab Nye (BOA Editions Ltd, 1994) reprinted here by kind permission of the author, Naomi Shihab Nye, 2018.

Nathalie Handal
'Echoes: A Historical Afterward', 'Here' and 'The Oranges', by Nathalie Handal (*This Week in Palestine*, Issue 227, March 2017); 'Bethlehem', 'Gaza City' and 'Jenin' by Nathalie Handal (Made in Palestine, October 2003). Reprinted here by kind permission of the author.

New York Review of Books
'Nothing More to Lose' from *Nothing More to Lose* © 2000, 2012, 2013, 2014 by Najwan Darwish, translation © 2014 by Kareem James Abu-Zeid (New York Review of Books, 2014). All rights reserved.

Penguin Random House
Excerpt from *Gate of the Sun* by Elias Khoury, translated from Arabic by Humphrey Davies published by Harvill Secker. Reproduced by permission of The Random House Group Ltd. © 2005

Ramzy Baroud
Excerpt from *The Last Earth: A Palestinian Story* by Ramzy Baroud (Pluto, 2018).

Remi Kanazi
'A Poem for Gaza', by Remi Kanazi, from www.remikanazi.com. 'Nakba', by Remi Kanazi, from *Before the Next Bomb Drops: Rising Up from Brooklyn to Palestine* (Haymarket Books, 2015).

Saqi Books
Excerpt from *The Lady from Tel Aviv* by Raba'i Al-Madhoun, translated by Eliott Colla (Telegram, 2013).

Sayed Kashua
'Memoire: On Nakba Day' by Sayed Kashua, excerpted from 'The Stories Sayed Kashua Wouldn't Dare Tell His Children' (*Haaretz*, 17 May 2012).

Smokestack Books
'I'm a Destitute Woman' by Maya Abu Al-Hayyat, translated by Maya Abu Al-Hayyat and Naomi Foyle; 'The Last of the Line of Refugee Descendants' translated by Jonathan Wright, 'Cracked Skin' and 'Being a Refugee' translated by Waleed Al-Bazoon and Naomi Foyle, by Ashraf Fayadh; 'Mimesis' by Fady Joudah; 'Everything in Our World Did Not Seem to Fit' by Naomi Shihab Nye; 'Resist, My People, Resist Them' translated by Tariq Haydar, and 'A Poet Behind Bars' translated by Tariq Haydar by Dareen Tatour; from *A Blade of Grass: New Palestinian Poetry*, edited by Naomie Foyle (Smokestack Books, 2018).

Tawfiq Zayyad
'We Shall Remain' by Tawfiq Zayyad, translated by Adib S. Kawar from *The Enemy of the Sun: Poetry of Palestinian Resistance* edited by Naseer Hasan Aruri and Edmund Ghareeb (Drum and Spear Press, 1970).

Taylor & Francis Group
'Man and His Alarm Clock' by Samira Azzam from *Middle Eastern Literatures*, 18:1, 86–92, Joseph R. Farag (Introduction), Wen-Chin Ouyang, Michael Beard & Nora E. Parr (Translation) (2015).

The American University in Cairo Press
Excerpt from *Mapping My Return: A Palestinian Memoir* by Salman Abu Sitta (The American University in Cairo Press, 2016).

The Operating System
'Being a Refugee' translated by Mona Kareem and Jonathan Wright, 'Cracked Skin' translated by Waleed Al-Bazoon and Naomi Foyle, and 'The Last of the Line of Refugee Descendants' translated by Jonathan Wright, from *Instructions Within* by Ashraf Fayadh (The Operating System, 2016). Reprinted with permission from The Operating System, Brooklyn, NY. Publisher/Editor Lynn DeSilva-Johnson.

The Permissions Company
'Exodus' by Taha Muhammad Ali, translated by Peter Cole, Yahya Hijazi and Gabriel Levin from *So What: New & Selected Poems 1971-2005* (Copper Canyon Press, 2006). Copyright © 2006 by Taha Muhammad Ali. Translation copyright © 2000, 2006 by Peter Cole, Yahya Hijazi, and Gabriel Levin. Reprinted with the permission of The Permissions Company, Inc., on behalf of Copper Canyon Press, www.coppercanyonpress.org.

The Wylie Agency
'Edward Said on his experience of the Nakba', copyright © 2000, Edward Said (*Democracy Now!* 16 October 2000), used by permission of The Wylie Agency (UK) Limited. 'Jerusalem Revisited' by Edward Said copyright © 1998, Edward Said (*Al-Ahram Weekly*, 'Special pages

commemorating 50 years of Arab dispossession since the creation of the State of Israel, 1998').

Verso Books
Excerpt from *In Search of Fatima: A Palestinian Story* by Ghada Karmi (Verso, 2002).

Yale University Press
'A Picture of The House in Beit Jala', 'Beirut, August 1982', 'Beyond That', 'Four Sisters from Zakariya' and 'Remembering the Grandmother' by Ghassan Zaqtan translated from Arabic by Fady Joudah, from *Like a Straw Bird It Follows Me: And Other Poems* (Yale University Press The Margellos World Republic of Letters, 2012).